SASQUATCH TRAVELS

Melissa George

Sasquatch Travels

By Melissa George

© Melissa George 2018

All rights reserved. No part of this publication may be reproduced, distributed, or transmitted in any form or by any means, including photocopying, copying, downloading, uploading, recording, or other electronic or mechanical methods, without the prior written permission of the publisher and/or Author.

Although the author and publisher have made every effort to ensure that the information in this book was correct at press time, the author and publisher do not assume and hereby disclaim any liability to any party for any loss, damage, or disruption caused by errors or omissions, whether such errors or omissions result from negligence, accident, or any other cause.

Cover Illustration Copyright © 2018 by Melissa George
Cover design by Melissa George
Book design and production by Melissa George
Images from Morgue file
Research and Verification by Cari S George, Melissa George, and Marty George

This is not a work of fiction. However, names and places in the book have been changed to keep the identity of the people involved in private.

Before I tell you our story, let me first say that I had never given any thought to Sasquatch. Of course, I had heard the term, but that was about as far as it went. I knew there was a show on TV called "Finding Bigfoot," but I had never seen it. I just didn't give any thought to UFO's or monsters. I was aware that some people did. But I was also aware that some people used drugs. I was as interested in one as I was the other. Neither had been a part of my life, and I was just fine with that.

My husband John and I owned a nice house in a well-established gated community. We had raised our daughter and put her through college. We both took early retirement from our community jobs and were comfortable. We had accomplished all of this without Sasquatch being a part of our lives. Now I wonder how we ever managed that one.

Looking back now, I wonder if we had just ignored it or if it was never brought up around us. I had never heard of Boggy Creek. And I was oblivious to Roger Patterson, Bob Gimlin, and Patty. Little did we know, that our retirement was about to throw us head over hills into a world that we never knew existed.

I have to say that I'm thankful for all that I have learned. And for being able to help as many people as we have. It would have been awful to have lived my life never knowing that these creatures were real. Or, that I could make a difference.

I know that we are certainly talked about behind our backs by close friends and family. I guess that's a given. But when you find out that they are really out there; there is an overwhelming need to tell others. Even though, that may not be the best or smartest thing to do.

Chapter 1

I was making a pot of coffee one afternoon when my neighbor Jan came over. As we sat and chatted, she mentioned her feet hurting. She explained that she and her husband had gone up to the state park the day before and hiked up to some waterfalls. She talked about how relaxing it was to get out into the woods and walk. She said some of the scenery was just breathtaking. While listening to her talk, I thought that this might be something John and I could do. The walking would be healthy for both of us, and it may be something we could start doing on a regular basis. Jan was happy to answer all of my questions. I had never considered us to be a hiking kind of couple, but it actually sounded kind of fun. I couldn't wait to talk to John about it.

That evening over dinner I mentioned what Jan and I had discussed. I could tell right away that John was considering the idea. I told him what Jan had said about the scenery is breathtaking. I knew that was something he would be interested in. We often went on long drives just to enjoy the view. And we could always get in a little fishing; I knew John wouldn't pass up the chance to go fishing. It was pretty simple to convince him that this was something we should try.

The next day was Saturday, so we drove to town to buy a few items for what I hoped would be our new hobby.

I thought our local sporting goods store would be the best place to start, but we somehow ended up at the Bass Pro Shop. This happens quite a lot actually, so I wasn't too surprised. John was always searching for a reason to be in there. And this was the golden ticket for him; he got to shop and spend some money. I happily tagged along behind. We bought hiking boots, backpacks a small tent and a double sleeping bag. I didn't think the tent and sleeping bag were necessary, but the salesman told us it was better to be safe than sorry. I just thought his sales were on commission.

To wind up our shopping trip, we ran by the grocery store for bottled water and snacks to take with us on our first hiking adventure. I was beginning to get excited.

We had planned our trip for the following Monday. We thought if we went during the week, there would be fewer people and we could take our time and enjoy all the park had to offer.

I had gotten our lunch ready Sunday afternoon, and I walked out to the garage to call John. I couldn't help but see what he was doing. I almost laughed right there on the kitchen steps but quickly thought better of it. There was no need in making him angry with me before our trip.

He struggled to try to attach his fishing pole to the backpack shelf as I quietly approached him.

"Lunch is on the table," I said. Not letting him know I had paid any attention to what he was doing.

"I'll be right there"; he mumbled laying down the fishing rod and moving toward his workbench.

I knew this 'hike" was going to turn into a fishing trip for him, and I was fine with that, knowing that he was trying to be discreet about it was really funny. By now, I knew him well enough to expect it. As I headed back to the kitchen, I called out over my shoulder," when you're done, would you fix my fishing rod to please"? I could hear him mumble under his breath. I laughed out loud this time. I knew that had been a few "not so nice" words directed toward me.

After seeing John with the fishing rod, I wondered if maybe we should take our little tent and sleeping bag. If the fish were biting good John wouldn't want to leave. I didn't mind fishing, but I wasn't as enthusiastic about it as John was. I would take a paperback book with me and be just fine while he fished the afternoon away. I would mention it to him during lunch.

The next morning, I was up before the sun and making coffee. I was really looking forward to spending a day in the woods, enjoying nature. Now that our daughter Tami had moved out and it was just the two of us, John and I didn't spend as much time getting out and doing things like we used to.

I had just finished scrambling some eggs and making toast when John came into the kitchen. I handed him a cup of coffee and said "good morning."

He looked at me with one raised eyebrow. "You're in a good mood," he said after taking a sip of his coffee.

"I'm excited about our hike today," I told him. "And I'm sure you're ready to do some fishing," I added.

"I can't argue with that," he responded. "It's been a while."

After breakfast, I cleaned the kitchen while John loaded the car. As I laced up my new hiking boots, I thought about taking my camera. I loved taking nature pictures and then sending them off to have them enlarged. I had framed landscapes all over the house. I had wanted something new to hang over the couch, and this might be the perfect opportunity. I grabbed my camera and some extra batteries as I headed out the door.

The state park was roughly an hour and a half from our house. The drive had been excellent, and the weather was perfect. It was a warm Autumn day. The warmth of summer was still trying to hang on, but the air was getting that familiar nip to it that let you know winter was just around the corner. I was glad that I had brought us each a light jacket.

John was non-stop talking for the whole drive. I could tell that he was excited about this fishing trip. I was excited for him, and I was looking forward to our hike. But something was nagging in the back of my mind. I kept trying to ignore it, but it was persistent; like the feeling, you get before something terrible happens. It wasn't a strong feeling, so I told myself that I was just being silly and tried to ignore it and enjoy the ride.

"You seem kind of quiet this morning," John said.

"I'm fine," I assured him. "I'm just enjoying the drive."

"I can't believe that we never thought to check out a state park before now," he continued." They have a lot of the outdoor things that we used to enjoy doing."
Maybe we just assumed they would always be crowded with tourist". He thought out loud.

"I know," I responded. "I guess it just never crossed our minds." But he was right. We did try to avoid the tourist crowds.

John turned on the radio to catch the morning news, and I was left to my own thoughts. I pushed the uneasy feeling to the back of my mind as I enjoyed the Autumn landscape. We pulled into a paved parking lot. There were only two other cars besides ours.

It looked like we had picked the right day.

There were some picnic tables under the trees at the far side of the parking lot and what appeared to be a general store with a quaint cabin look to it. It had a sign on the front that said office. I assumed this must be the ranger station. This was all new to me.

We parked the car and grabbed our gear before walking up to the Office. John thought it might be a good idea for us to stop and see if we needed to check in. Weren't you supposed to check in? Isn't that how they knew if someone got lost? Oh great. In all of my excitement, I hadn't thought about that. And this really wasn't the best time to be feeling this way. I tried to push the thought to the back of my mind.

The ranger station was set to resemble a small cabin. Complete with a front porch and rocking chairs. As John opened the door, a bell sounded over the top announcing our arrival. The smell of fresh coffee greeted us. I knew right away that this was my kind of place. I had every intention of locating the source of this lovely smell before we left.

A voice from the back called out "Come on in and make yourself at home. I'll be with you in a moment." The voice came from an older, gray-haired man just past the counter. He was busy hanging some flyers on a bulletin board.

John called back, "Thank you, Sir." As we began to browse the store; I was shocked to see the vast assortment of things they carried. There were camping and fishing gear along with food and snacks. There were Ice chests and fold out lounge chairs along with bear spray and mosquito repellant. If you left anything behind, you could easily buy it here. I bet they made a killing out of sheer convenience.

We finally made our way over to the register and was greeted with a warm smile as John sat a tub of worms on the counter.

"You two planning on doing some fishing today"? The man asked as he rang up John's purchase. I had moved down the counter to the coffee pot as John, and the ranger talked about fishing. The ranger was telling him about a good spot that was just off of the main trail.

I fixed my coffee and walked over just as he was handing John some pamphlets on the hiking trails. He gave me a warm smile and told me that he hoped we enjoyed our day. He said that there was a large book on a table by the door and asked if we would please sign it before we entered the park. This must be how they kept up with people. So I had been right.

As John and I stopped to sign the book, the ranger told us that the trail started just past the picnic tables and the trails were clearly marked all the way through the park. We thanked him and headed out.

As we walked back across the parking lot, I thought that this backpack was more than I had bargained for. I think we should have gone with the day packs I had wanted to get. They had looked more like a kids backpack. But John had let the young salesman talk him into going with the full gear. I was already regretting that decision. Nearing the car, I was wondering how I should tell John that this big pack was just a little too much for me. Luckily, I didn't have to.

"Let's stop by the car for a minute," John said. "I have an idea."

We walked up to the back of the car with both of us unshouldering the heavy packs. "Wait right here," He said. He headed back to the Ranger station at a brisk pace.

It wasn't long before I looked up and saw John coming back across the parking lot. I couldn't help but laugh as he held up two shoulder bags! He was grinning from ear to ear.
"I think these will work better for us," he said with a laugh. We took our snacks and bottled water out of the big backpacks and placed them in our small ones. I dropped my camera and batteries inside as John freed our fishing poles. We shouldered the lightweight packs. Grabbed our fishing poles and headed off.

We quickly found the trail and entered the woods. I was immediately surrounded by the smell of damp earth and leaf litter. It had been a long time since I had smelled this and it instantly soothed me. I had forgotten just how much I loved the smell of the woods.

As we walked the birds sang overhead, and squirrels darted back and forth across the forest floor. It was so very peaceful. I could get used to this. There were no other sounds except for the occasional rustle of the trees as the light winds played with the branches. I felt like I could stay here forever.

I wasn't paying attention to how far we had walked. I was just enjoying the weather and being outdoors when John stopped. "This has to be the trail the Ranger was telling me about," he said. Looking at what appeared to be a small footpath.

I didn't think this was it at all. This looked like something animals would use instead of people. I had an image of us getting lost in the park. I thought back to the news stories I had heard where people had to have rescuers come out and look for them. Yep. That would be us.

"Are you sure"? I asked him doubtfully. "It doesn't look like much of a trail."

John looked around." We have come about two miles already", he said. "The ranger said the trail was about two miles in and to the left. He also said that if we weren't looking for it, we would miss It".

I looked down at my watch. We had been walking just a little past an hour.

"Let's give it a try," John said, walking onto the little path. "After a little way, if we don't think this is it, we will just turn around and come back."

I still didn't think this was it, but I couldn't argue with his reasoning. "OK," I agreed reluctantly. I followed him down the small path.

The narrow trail led down into the thick woods. It didn't look like this path was used much at all. I kept telling myself that we wouldn't get lost if we stayed on the trail. But I wasn't making myself feel any better; as we followed this path in between the trees and through the ever-thickening brush. I'm not sure how far we had walked when I noticed how much quieter the woods were here. The birds had stopped, and I didn't see any squirrels at all.

"It sure is quiet in here," I told John. I even lowered my voice as I spoke. It just seemed like the rational thing to do.

"I thought that myself," John said. "It's almost like we walked into some completely different woods."

We continued to walk with me following John. I was now paying more attention to where I was putting my feet. The terrain was not as smooth as the trail we had initially been on, and It would be easy to twist an ankle. I was thinking this and didn't see that John had stopped. I walked right into the back of him almost causing us both to tumble over the downed tree on our path. My lack of attention and the fact that I rammed him pretty hard caused John to have a few choice words for me.

" Dad blame it, Susan! Can you please watch where you're going"!?

I stepped back to get off of him and apologized. "I'm sorry, I responded. "I was looking down and didn't see you stop." John let out an irritated sigh. I wasn't sure why he was irritated, but I wasn't about to ask him. Maybe he was just anxious to find the lake, so he could fish.

Looking at the tree, John said; "This doesn't make any sense." I wasn't sure what he was talking about. Trees fell in the forest all the time. What made this one so different?

"What is it"? I asked curiously. It looked like a regular tree to me.

"We haven't had any bad storms lately," he said; studying the tree.

"What do you mean"? I asked, still not understanding what he was getting at. What was the big deal?

John looked at me as he spoke. "This tree didn't just fall down Susan," he said. "Take a look at this," he said, pointing toward the roots. "They are still green. This tree was alive when it fell."

Now I could see what he meant. This tree had been pushed or pulled over somehow. But How? And why? John was right. This didn't make any sense. Why would someone make an effort to fell this tree and then just leave it here? It was a rather large tree so it couldn't have been easy to cut it.

"It hasn't been here long. The leaves are barely wilted. This had to have come down earlier this morning." John said: still studying the tree.

"It is strange," I agreed.

"well, looks like we get off the trail a bit," John said with a laugh.

We skirted around the tree pushing our way through some thick underbrush. This hike was beginning to be more work than fun I thought.

By the time we found the lake I was hot, sweaty and tired. It was well past lunch, and I was starving.

John looked around to find us a nice place to sit. That wasn't an easy task as most of the underbrush grew clear to the bank. I can see why the ranger said that this would be a nice place for fishing. If you didn't know it was here, you would never find it!

As I stood there examining my skin for scratches and thorns, I heard John call from a distance. "Over here Susan, I found a nice spot!"

I looked up in the direction his voice had come from. I saw nothing but trees and more thick underbrush. Great! I was going to have to fight my way over there. I let out a sigh and begin to shoulder through the brush.

After what seemed like forever, I came out close to where John was. He was right! It was lovely here. There was a small beach that sloped right down to the water. It was actually sandy with no undergrowth.

Someone had been here before us because there were four V-shaped sticks that were still stuck into the ground by the water. Apparently, they had been used to hold fishing rods.

As I looked around, I realized that there was nowhere to sit except for the ground. I looked for the nearest tree that maybe I could sit by. But all of the trees were surrounded by brush. Oh well, it seemed like this wasn't going to be as relaxing as I had hoped it would.

John had unshouldered his backpack and sat down beside it; as he unzipped it and started pulling things out. He looked up at me and smiled. Sarcastically, he said, "grab a chair and have a seat."

I realized then that he was happy to be out here and this had all been my idea. The least I could do was not complain. I smiled back and resigned myself to just be uncomfortable for a little while. I sat down on the dirt beside him. I was looking forward to the food I had packed for us.

An hour later John was happily fishing the afternoon away, and I was as bored as could be. I had tried reading for a while but with nowhere to get comfortable, it was difficult to concentrate on my book. I got up and walked around. That didn't take long as the clearing we were in was pretty small. I sat down next to John with a sigh.

John reached over into his backpack. Pulling out a black square case, he said, "here," handing it to me.

"What's this"? I asked opening the case. I pulled out a pair of shiny black binoculars.

I put the binoculars up to my eyes and looked out across the lake. This was pretty neat. I spent some time bird watching and then I watched a couple of deer come down to the water for a drink. I had forgotten that John even had these. We had bought them years ago on one of our trips into the Great Smokey Mountains. They had been perfect for watching the Bear and Elk. Now they would entertain me while John fished.

I had sat the Binoculars down while I got bottled water and a pack of crackers from my backpack. Just as I lifted up my bottle to take a drink, I saw something on the other side of the lake. I couldn't make out what it was, and by the time I put my bottle down and picked up the binoculars it had moved back into the trees. I assumed it was a bear. It had seemed pretty big and was dark in color. By adjusting the binoculars, I caught a glimpse of the fur just inside the tree line. It had to be a bear. Usually, this would worry me. John was fishing, and that could bring an unwanted bear into our area. But today John was just catching and releasing. We didn't have any fresh fish on a stringer.

"I think there is a bear across the lake," I told John.

He asked if it had cubs. I told him that I hadn't seen any and it went back into the trees before I had a good look. He told me it was fine and not to worry. He didn't see any reason for it to want to check us out.

I put the binoculars down and lay back on the ground. The sun had felt good, but some clouds were starting to come in now. It looked like we might get some rain soon.
As if reading my mind John stood up and began to put his things away. This was my signal to get my own gear together.

I wasn't looking forward to the walk back out. Fighting through the brush was bad enough, but now it looked like we might get rained on as well. What in the world had ever made me think that I would enjoy hiking? Right now I had rather be home in my recliner reading a good book. But here I was shouldering through the dense underbrush as the first raindrops began to fall. The temperature had dropped too, and my little windbreaker was not enough.
It seemed like we had been walking for hours, but my watch told me that it had only been forty-five minutes when John stopped. The rain was still coming down in a fine mist; I hesitantly asked him what was wrong.

Without turning to look at me, he said, "I seem to have lost the trail."

I felt my heart fall to my feet. I knew it! I knew this was going to happen when we first walked off the main trail. This is how it always happens. People get off the main trail thinking they can easily find their way back and then they are lost and walking for days; bleeding feet and eating grasshoppers!

"Excuse me"? I muttered.

"I thought we would be to the downed tree by now," he said with a sigh.

"We haven't walked long enough," I told him with excitement in my voice. I explained to him that we had only been walking just under an hour and it had taken us nearly an hour to find the lake once we passed the tree.

"Are you sure"? John asked looking relieved;

"I'm positive I told him" with a smile. I was feeling rather proud of myself. I wouldn't be eating grasshoppers tonight after all! We continued on a little further before we came across the fallen tree. John led the way around the top of it. The same way we had walked earlier.

The rain was becoming a little heavier. It wasn't a full blown rain storm yet, but it was more substantial than the mist we were getting earlier. Just as we rounded the top of the tree, John stopped once again.

I was just about to ask him what was wrong this time when he spun around, instantly and firmly placing his hand over my mouth. He leaned in close to my ear and whispered:

"Don't make a sound." I nodded my head in agreement as my heart leaped up into my throat. It had to be a bear! As John released me, I saw past his shoulder the object of his concern.

Something was in the brush just to the right of the trail and only about twenty feet away. It looked like the back side of a black bear. It had it's back to us as it stood there unmoving. I prayed it would just move on into the brush. The last thing we needed was to surprise a bear.

And then suddenly everything I had ever believed in came crashing down around me. My world stopped turning at the same moment that my brain shuddered and froze.

This bear stood up! It had to be eight foot tall. And that estimate is allowing for my fear, my uncertainty and my lack of rational thinking.

This thing stood up and turned completely around to look at us. The tall grass that had almost been to the top of its back was now about knee height.

My eyes and my brain were no longer communicating. I was looking into a face that was almost human. Its expression led me to believe that it was as surprised or maybe even as scared as I was. We stood there in the rain; all three of us just looking at each other. This thing was the color of a black bear. The skin on its face was dark with the fur stopping at the edges. Its forehead protruded a little further than ours with a flared nose. The eyes were much larger than ours and very dark. The lips were thin on its full mouth. The head was much bigger than ours with the hair on top looking like a short Mohawk. The shoulders were massive with tapering arms that seemed to stop just below the knees. The fur covered the backs of the giant hands. Its waist was slightly narrower leading to very muscular legs. The anatomy of a male species was present.

I just stood there in the rain looking at this creature as all of my senses shut down. This wasn't real. I was dreaming and would wake up in my own bed shortly.

This creature moved its head slightly as if to sniff the wind, and my reality came rushing back almost causing me to scream. I knew in my mind that I was standing there in the middle of a State Park, in the rain looking at something that didn't exist. I was looking at a Sasquatch.

The rain suddenly began to fall harder. And this Sasquatch turned away from us, almost as if he had lost interest and disappeared into the woods. I didn't realize that I had been holding my breath until It came rushing out. Without saying a word John grabbed my hand and quickly pulled me up the trail. My head was still spinning. But everything in me wanted out of these woods. That thing could easily kill both of us with minimal effort: and I didn't want to run into it again.

John and I came out onto the main trail at almost a run. Without speaking, we hurried back down the path to the car. Once we made it back to the parking lot the rain had turned into a downpour and ours was the only car on the lot. John unlocked my door before hurrying around the vehicle to his own. I was wet and cold when I climbed into the front seat, but all I could think about was that face, that huge black face.

Chapter 2

Thirty minutes later we sat in our car at a fast food restaurant with hot coffee. At this point, neither of us had spoken. We both were taking cautious sips of the coffee: when John finally said. "It's still hard to wrap your head around it, isn't it"?

I said softly, almost hesitantly, "Tell me what you saw John. What was that thing back there"?

After a few seconds, John took a deep breath and said, "Susan, the only way I know how to describe that thing is to call it a Sasquatch."

I knew what he meant. That had to be what it was. But my mouth wasn't ready to say that word yet.

"But they don't exist," I said softly. Tears were beginning to fill up my eyes. Monsters were now real, and I wasn't sure how to handle this realization.

"They didn't yesterday," John said. "But what I just saw back there in those woods was a Sasquatch." He said with certainty.

"How do you feel about that"? I asked; as we both watched the rain rivers running down the windshield.

"I'm still not sure." He said. "I've got to have time to think about this." I nodded my head in agreement. That's what I needed; I needed some time to think.

On the drive home, John and I did a lot of speculating. I asked John if there was any way possible that this could have been someone in a costume trying to scare us. He told me that he had considered this, but there was no way anyone could be that tall. I had been thinking the same thing. I was just trying to find a way to rationalize what I had seen.

"But if we saw a Sasquatch, that means others have seen it too," I said. That means that the people that run the park would have to know that it's out there, right"? I asked John.

"Possibly," John said. "But I have a feeling that if they do know anything, they aren't going to talk."

"But why wouldn't they"? I asked. Suddenly confused. "Shouldn't they need to warn people"?

"Think about the bigger picture Susan" was John's response. If the park rangers agree that there is a Sasquatch living in the state park do you realize what kind of chaos that would bring about? For one, these things haven't been proven to exist. The media would have a field day, and on the flip side it would scare the be-jesus out of most of America".

Wow! John was right. I hadn't thought about any of this. Now, this brought the question to mind. Does our government know they exist? And if so, what were they gaining about keeping it quiet?

This whole thing was beginning to be mind-boggling. This morning I had been excited to go hiking. Now my entire world had changed.

The rest of the drive home was John and I both bouncing ideas and theories back and forth. At the time, neither of us knew anything about Sasquatch. But that was about to change for both of us.

Once we got home, we both showered and changed into dry clothes. I went to make us some warm soup while John turned on the laptop at the kitchen counter. We both had a million questions, and the best place for us to get answers would be the internet. A simple search of the word Sasquatch brought up tons of information, websites, pictures, and video. How in the world would we ever sort through all of this?

We watched a couple of the videos while we ate. Then spent the rest of the night trying to read through the seemingly endless websites. There was so much information that I finally got out a notebook and started writing things down.

We were shocked to find out just how many people were aware of these creatures and had seen them just like we had. There were literally hundreds of people that called themselves Bigfoot or Sasquatch researchers. They devoted a lot of time and energy looking for these seemingly elusive creatures. Many had never seen one, but they had found "evidence" that they had been in the area. John and I were online until well after midnight and had barely scratched the surface. We had unknowingly walked into a whole different world.

The next day John was scheduled to go play golf with some of the men in the neighborhood. Most of the retirees that lived in our community was a lot older than John and me. So John would go with them to play Golf and they in return would go on fishing trips with John. I think it was more the case that they tolerated the fishing trips. But they would happily follow him along as long as he was going golfing and bowling with them.

John left for his golfing trip very reluctantly. He had almost called twice to cancel. He was feeling the same way I was. There was a burning need to find out more about the Sasquatch. Like John. It was on my mind when I woke up, and I couldn't wait to start learning more about it.

I waited until Joh had left the house before turning on the computer. I felt that it would have been cruel of me to do it while he was home knowing that he wanted to do this as bad as I did.

I began to learn about tree structures, tree knocks and some of the howls that these creatures were reported to make. The more I learned, the more I wanted to get out in the woods and experience these things for myself. Yet the thought of going back up to the park sort of unnerved me. I wanted to have these experiences and learn all I could about these things. But they were scary big and as unpredictable as any wild animal. If one of them decided to attack you; there wouldn't be a whole lot you could do to protect yourself. That was the part that scared me.

I took some notes on what to look for. And there were a few items I needed to add to our day packs. I wasn't only learning about Sasquatch, but I was picking up some great hiking tips too. I could take some orange tape to mark our trail into the woods. And carry a whistle in case we got lost. Many things like this just screamed common sense. We would be more prepared this time.

I didn't realize how much time I had spent online until John came in through the kitchen door. I quickly looked up at the clock. It was going on four. I needed to get up and start some dinner.

"Did you learn anything"? John asked.

"Oh yes!" I exclaimed. " But I don't think we will ever weed through all of the information that's out there," I said with a sigh.

"That's a good thing," John said. "That means we will keep learning as we go." He removed his jacket and hung it by the door before claiming my now vacant stool.

Once again we ate dinner watching Youtube videos. I asked John how he felt about going back to the state park. He gave me a serious look. " I'm shocked that you even asked me that, " he said. " I thought it would be like pulling teeth for me get you back up there. Are you seriously considering it?" he asked.

I told him that I really wasn't looking forward to ever seeing that creature again. Yet there was something burning inside me. I just had to know more. I had to go back to that spot. I didn't know what I would do when I got there. Look for evidence? I had no idea. I just knew that I felt a strong need to go.

We made plans that evening to go back the next day. I lay in bed that night picturing a thousand different outcomes for tomorrow. I was both scared and excited at the same time. I wanted to go and look for things like footprints, broken trees and stick structures. But the thought of seeing this creature again scared me. If it decided to attack, there would be nothing you could do to defend yourself. Absolutely nothing.

The only thing I could think of that might have a chance of dropping one of these creatures would be a high powered rifle or a strong tranquilizer. And of course, we had neither of these. I scooted over against Johns back. We would see what tomorrow holds together. For tonight, I was safe.

The next morning we got up early and threw some things into our lightweight day packs. I found some bright orange tape out in the garage. But I didn't have a whistle. It was not something I really needed anyway. This time, I put the cords on both the camera and the binoculars. John could carry one while I took the other. I thought that by wearing them around our necks, we could get to them quickly if we needed to.

The day was supposed to be warm and sunny. But it was still dark when we left the house. We had hoped to get there early and take our time looking around. Then once we got home, we could compare our findings to those on the internet.

The drive didn't seem to take nearly as long this time. Before I knew it, John was driving into the parking lot. This time he parked right in front of the trailhead. We would have to walk all the way across the parking lot to check in at the ranger station, and that was fine with me. By parking near the trailhead, if something happened out there, it would be quicker getting to the car.

As we walked across the parking lot, the sun was just beginning to burn away the morning fog. It held the promise of a lovely fall day. The leaves were starting to turn, and the woods were just beautiful. I was still feeling a little nervous, but I knew this was something we had to do.

A younger man greeted us this time when we entered the building. I was once again hit with the pleasant aroma of fresh coffee.

"Good morning," came a friendly call from the counter. "The coffee is fresh if you would like some." This man wore the same familiar brown clothing the last one wore. But he was a good twenty years younger.

'Thank you!" John called back as we made our way over to the counter. This time he joined me in a large cup of the aromatic coffee".

We took our cups over to the register on the counter. I could see now that the man's name tag said, Brett. "Oh, there is no charge for the coffee," Brett said, keeping the same friendly smile. And we keep it going all day, so feel free to come back if you want to."

"Thank you," John said with a laugh. My wife just may take you up on that".

"You just come back when you're ready," Brett said, smiling at me.

"So, are you guys here to hike, camp or fish"? Brett asked, turning his attention back to John.

"We thought we might do a little nature hiking," John replied. "I think it's going to be a nice day for it."

"Brett went into his well-trained salesman pitch. "Well, we have Granola bars and trail mix along with some Slim Jims and dried jerky." He said motioning us toward the food items.

"I think I'll have a look," John replied. I wondered why in the world he wanted to buy food when we had food in our packs. But I followed him over to the food aisle. John must have seen the confused look on my face."Trust me", he said softly, as he picked up a few granola bars and some Venison Jerkey packs.

John paid for our snacks as Brett told him where the trees were the prettiest and how to get to a couple of scenic waterfalls. John pretended to be interested in the advice he was giving us on how to get the most of our day hike.

We both thanked him and headed over to the guest registry with our still warm coffee.

Once we got away from the front of the ranger station, John explained to me why he had purchased the snacks. He had read online a few things about leaving the Sasquatch treats.

We grabbed our backpacks from the car and headed for the trail while John explained to me the theory behind gifts and habituation. I remembered seeing a couple of articles on this, but I hadn't really read them. I was now thankful that John had bought the extra snacks. If there was anything we could do to keep this creature from being angry, then I was all for it!

It didn't take us long to find the small path this time. John remembered where it was. Once we entered the path, our pace slowed down a lot. I think we had hurried because we were so eager to see if we could find anything, but once we got on the smaller path, we were both unsure. I noticed that neither of us was speaking, almost as if we were holding our breath.

John came to a sudden stop, but this time I didn't bump into him. I had been keeping an eye on my surroundings. I stepped up to his side to see what he was looking at. About fifty yards ahead of us was the fallen tree. It was looking much more withered now. But it was still laying there across the trail. This was when I realized that the woods had gone silent again.

"go ahead and get your tape out," John said as he scanned the woods around us with his binoculars. I wasn't sure what he had in mind. But I immediately unshouldered my backpack and dug out the tape for him. As I handed him the tape, he told me to start turning in a small circle and snap random photos of the woods. I still wasn't sure what he was up to, but I did as he asked.

As I snapped random photos, John walked over to a small tree just a few feet away from us and tied the tape around it. I wondered why he would mark the path. We knew how to find our way back to this spot. "Follow me," he said with a smile as he cut to the right off of the path. This looked like it was going to lead us up a small slope. But I trusted John, so I followed him. I felt a lot better knowing that we were marking our progress with the tape. Every so often John would stop and tie the tape around a small tree. He was putting it about head level so it would be easier to see.

We hadn't gone far off the path when John stopped and said, "Would you look at that"? Right in front of us was what had to be a tree structure. There were random sticks and branches all stood on their end around a tree. It looked like something a kid might do trying to make a teepee.

As we examined this more closely, I realized that there was no possible way a kid or a group of kids could have done this. These branches were from many different trees. There were no drag marks on the ground where someone could have drug them here. The ground was heavily packed down about four feet completely around this structure. You could easily see where something had walked around the tree while creating this. But there were no definite footprints. The leaf litter was just too thick, whatever had done this didn't leave any prints. I was fascinated. It was possible that the creature we had seen the other day had created this. But why? What was the purpose?

I slowly walked in a circle taking random pictures of this while John got down on his knees and examined it more closely. As John stood back up, he said, "come over here and look at this." I put my camera down and went to see what he was talking about.

John pointed out that the majority of these branches had been twisted and broken off. They weren't just found on the forest floor and brought here. They had first been broken out of trees and then brought here, seeing this caused a strange feeling in my stomach.

I knew this had been done by a very powerful creature, that could be watching us right now. The hair stood up on the back of my neck. I looked up into the woods half expecting to see it standing there. But what I saw instead was a broken tree limb. A tree that was about five foot from us had a twisted and broken branch. I was more than ready to move on. As if reading my mind, John said, "let's go." He tied another piece of tape to a nearby tree. He then laid out two sections of the Venison Jerkey and a granola bar on top of the structure. And we moved on into the woods.

As we walked, we came into a small clearing. The ground was void of any leaf litter here. The slope allowed the rainwater to keep the leaves washed away in this area. John stopped walking before he ever stepped out into the opening. "Be really careful here," he said. "We may be able to find some prints. So watch where you're stepping."

I painstakingly watched every footstep as I slowly moved around the clearing. I was finding animal tracks that John pointed out were mostly deer. But there were a few Opossum and a few coyotes. I'm personally not a big fan of the coyote.

I have heard them howl before and it sent shivers down my spine. It has to be one of the creepiest sounds I have ever heard. And it's my mindset that if they can take down large prey: what would stop them from attacking a human? Knowing there was coyote out here didn't make me as uneasy as the Sasquatch. I knew the coyote mostly hunted at night, so the probability of running into one didn't bother me.
I straightened up and rubbed my back. "I do not see anything at all," I told John.

"Neither have I," he said, Straightening his back too. "I was hoping to find something," he said with a sigh.

We picked up our backpacks and continued on through the woods. We walked for quite a while not seeing anything. But just before we walked back out into the clearing by the lake, we came across another structure. This one was entirely different from the one we had seen earlier. There was a large tree that was the central part of the structure. This large tree had a V shape where another tree was balanced perfectly in the V; there were smaller trees that had been broken off and propped against the balanced tree. This was not anything that was done by kids or nature. I immediately took my camera from around my neck and began snapping pictures as John examined it closer. Just like the first structure, there were no footprints in the leaf litter. It was only packed down where something had walked.

John and I sat on the sandy ground by the lake and ate our lunch. We were both thrilled for finding the structures. It only helped to verify that what we saw was real and was in these woods.

I had hoped to see a footprint. But knowing this was our first time out, I couldn't expect to see everything at one time. We were lucky to have come across the two structures.
I asked John what direction we were going in next. He said he thought we would head around the edge of the lake if I were up to fighting through the underbrush. I immediately looked down at my watch. This made John laugh.

"I promised to have you back at the car before dark, and I will," he said with a smile.

I just didn't want to be walking around in these woods in the dark knowing this thing was out here. That thought caused goosebumps to pop up on my arms now. While rubbing my arms, I looked out across the lake. I told him that sounded fine. He stood up and offered me his hand.

For the next little while, we were fighting our way through the underbrush. I began to think that this had been a bad idea. There was no way we were going to find anything out here. I finally stopped walking and asked. "Is there some sort of plan to this"?

John stopped and looked back at me. "I was hoping to find another area near the water that didn't have as many leaves. I'm sorry the going has been pretty tough".

"It's OK, I told him with a smile. Let's go on a little further and see how it goes." He was trying his best to make this easy on me. I couldn't blame him for us being out here it had been my idea.

We weren't going to find any good evidence by staying on the trail. I knew this before we ever came. I had only questioned him so I would know what his plan was.

After what seemed like forever, we did finally make it onto another sandy part of the lake. From here, you could see the campground on the far side. John immediately started checking the ground. I sat my backpack at the edge of the woods and began looking too. It was only a minute before John called out "Susan! I found some!"

I hurried over to where he stood. There was a massive footprint in the sand! And right up against this big one was a small one that had to be from a young Sasquatch! I couldn't believe what I was seeing! My heart began to race as I carefully studied the prints.

"Oh my God, John," I exclaimed! "There was a baby!"

John had dropped to his knees and was digging something out of his backpack. He brought out a tape measure and laid it beside the print. The tape read sixteen inches long and five inches across! The smaller one was six inches by two and a half. This had to have been a female with her baby.

John laid the tape measure back on the ground beside the big print and told me to get some pictures. In my excitement, I had forgotten all about my camera

As I began to snap photos from many different angles, John tracked the prints back to the edge of the woods. By the way the footprints were, it appeared that the mother had carried her young to the edge of the water and sat it down. She then picked it back up and returned to the woods. The smaller prints were only found at the edge of the water. Had she brought it here to drink, or to bathe it? As exciting as this find was, it only brought more questions.

This had got my adrenaline pumping, and I was ready to go further. I wanted to find more. John felt the same way, but we decided it would be best to leave some treats and head back. We had hoped to make it home before dark, and we still had a long walk out and then a long drive home.

John pulled the plastic bag containing the treats out of his backpack. He took everything out of the bag and laid it on the ground. He gathered some large pieces of Venison Jerkey and two granola bars to place back in the plastic bag. The rest he dropped into his backpack. "Now to find a tree to hang this from," He said looking toward the woods.

I asked why he was going to hang it since he had left the last treats on top of the structure. He said that if a mother was moving through here with her young, he wanted to make sure she could get to it instead of the other wildlife. This made perfect sense to me. So John had learned a few tricks by reading online too.

I quickly dug into my backpack and grabbed two apples to be added to her bag. I just hoped the female would find this bag for her and her baby.

John and I bent down a small tree and tied the bag near the top. Once the tree stood back up, the bag was easily eight feet off the ground. That should keep most of the other wildlife away. We both picked up our bags and began the long walk out.

Walking out I seemed to tire easier than when we walked in. I guess the excitement of the day had worn off and now I was feeling each step. John reminded me to keep my eyes open for signs as we headed out. I had needed that reminder. I caught myself watching my feet more than looking around us.

When we finally made it back to the first structure, I was more than ready for a break! We had picked up the pace on the way out, and I was feeling it. As we neared the structure, I was straining my eyes to see if the treats we had left were still there. When I could finally see that they were, I felt disappointed. I was hoping that the Sasquatch had found them and taken them. But in reality, that thing could be hundreds of miles from here today. I let out a sigh and followed John back to the main trail.

Chapter 3

We were both anxious to find out if anything took our bag. But we would have to wait a while before we would have the chance to go back. We each had other things that we needed to take care of. We were still spending as much time as we could online but, like any hobby, we had to limit ourselves while we took care of our other commitments.

Each evening, we would have our dinner at the kitchen counter as we watched YouTube videos. We were learning a lot from the videos that other researchers were putting up there. It wasn't long before we found out that there was a whole world of Bigfoot researchers and they had taken social media by storm. If you knew where to look, you could find a treasure trove of information. But just like anything else, this had its bad points too. There were so many people putting information out there that it was hard to tell what was true and what wasn't. And unfortunately, that can do a lot of harm to new-comers in this field. We decided that the best we could do was to hang back, and read what others were saying, then pick and choose what we deemed believable. (I would advise anyone new to this field to do the same.) It also helped us in making the decision not to put any of our findings on the internet. If we kept our evidence to ourselves, for now, we would be much better off. I uploaded my images to the computer and kept them in a folder on the hard drive.

I came down with a cold in the first part of November. So that kept us from going back to the park for a couple of weeks. By the time I was feeling better, the weather had turned cold. John and I wore thick sweatshirts under our winter coats as we loaded into the car before sun up. I was seriously wondering if this trip was going to do any good. The bag was probably long gone by now. I'm sure some kind of wildlife would have found a way to get into it.

I was looking forward to seeing if there were any new structures. But I wasn't sure if that excitement outweighed the long walk in the cold.

When we arrived at the park, I felt sure we would be the only ones there, and we were. Not many people want to go hiking when it's this cold, plus the fact that the winter landscape isn't all that pretty. Bare trees with dead leaves and a sky that looked like it would open up and pour at any minute. We weren't supposed to get any rain, but I have known a weatherman to be wrong before.

I was looking forward to a steaming cup of coffee as we walked across the parking lot.

John purchased two bags of Venison Jerkey, and we had our usual friendly chat with the Park Ranger. It was the same elderly gentleman we had seen on our first trip out here. His name tag said, Joe. I wondered why I hadn't noticed that the first time.

Joe gave us a peculiar look when John told him that we would be hiking for a while. But he smiled once John said to him that the fresh air was good for his bronchitis, and the walking kept us feeling young.

This time, when we got back to the car to shoulder our backpacks, I didn't leave my coffee behind. I was carrying it with me like it was precious gold. When John saw mine, he decided that he would take his too. It would be a great hand warmer, at least for a little while.

John walked us all the way to the fallen tree this time, and then we walked into the direction it had been pushed from. His idea was to walk a full circle ending up at the place where we left the bag.

We didn't see any structures that we could be sure of, but we did see a few things that were odd. On one tree, there was a large branch shoved down into a knothole at the base of it. Then two very tall trees seemed to be propped against each other. Like they were using each other for support. But I guess the wind could have done this.

As we neared the lake, John pointed out something to me. "Look at this Susan," he said, pointing to a bent tree. I didn't understand what he was showing me. To me, it was just a twisted tree. Sometimes a tree would grow in a bent shape. I didn't see anything out of the ordinary.

And then John pointed to the top of the tree. I walked over and was shocked to see that it was held down by a large rock.

"What does it mean?" I asked, looking up at John.

"I'm not really sure," he responded. They say this is done by the Sasquatch. Some say they do this to mark water sources and some say they are their trail markers. But either way, they all believe that they are created by the Sasquatch. They call them Arches."

I agreed that they must be done by the Sasquatch. What purpose would it serve for a human to do this? Now I was feeling a little better about our walk today. I snapped a few pictures before we moved on.

The rest of the walk was uneventful. The cloud cover made it feel damp, and the wind was picking up. My nose was utterly frozen. I wanted to learn about these creatures, but was it really worth it?

We came out of the brush a little further down the lake than where we had tied up our bag. Luckily, we were still on the sandy part and didn't have to go through more dead bushes.

As we neared where the bag had been hung, I could see something white on the ground. It was the bag! John picked it up to examine it. It looked like it had been torn into. Not chewed into, but ripped into.

The top was still tied, but the side was torn out. Near where the bag had laid was a single Granola wrapper, and again, it had been torn into. There were no teeth marks anywhere on it. How could a regular animal manage this? They would have to use their teeth to get the package open, wouldn't they? This fascinated both of us. John and I lay the bag and wrapper back where we had found them for me to get some pictures. We then picked them up and put them in a Ziploc bag in Johns backpack. While John was busy with cleaning up, I snapped some random pictures around the lake. I had learned that you could never take to many photos.

John pulled another bag out of his backpack and placed a sealed bag of Venison Jerky in it. We then added two apples and four Granola bars. We tied this bag back to the tree just like we had done the first one, but this time, John kicked away the leaves underneath the tree in hopes that we would get some good prints.

With this done, it was time to start the long walk back out. Just as John shouldered his backpack, a tree knock came from across the lake!

We both spun around as if something would be standing right behind us. As we stood there looking out across this vast lake, another knock came from the same area. It's one thing to hear these over your computer speakers, but to hear one while you're out in the woods is fantastic. It actually sent shivers down my spine. There was no doubt now, that one was close by.

"Do you think we should knock back"? I asked.

John checked the woods for a stick big enough to give a solid knock with. He counted to three and whacked a nearby tree with the stick. It sounded just like what we had heard! We waited while straining our ears for the faintest sound! After a couple of minutes hearing nothing, we decided it was time to leave.

I was pleased with the way things had gone today. We both got validation that we weren't crazy and that there was actually something out there. I was already looking forward to rechecking the bag, and we had barely left the park.

Later that evening, I loaded the pictures from my camera onto the computer. I always found this interesting. There was a chance that I may have caught something. I hadn't so far, but it was still fun to check them. We had gone through most of them, and there was nothing questionable. But when we got to the ones I had taken by the lake. There was something odd 0n one of the photos. About fifty yards from us, there was a dark area in between two trees. In my next picture of the same area, there was nothing between the same two trees. There was no way we could make out what it was. It was just too far away. But there was definitely something there. It's funny how a dark blob between two trees can excite you, but it did. This was the strange people we were becoming.

As it turned out, John and I didn't make it back out to the park for another six weeks. Things in our daily lives again seemed to take over, and we just couldn't find the time.

While we waited for an opportunity to get out to the park, we were both still studying all we could. I had even ordered some books that had been written by some credible people. We were getting better at weeding out the frauds and the jokers. I was getting really good at taking notes.

The more we studied about Bigfoot/Sasquatch, the stranger things got. We had subscribed to a few Podcasts and enjoyed listening to other peoples encounters. But, other people were experiencing some strange stuff out there in the woods, or they were just plain lying. But I had to wonder why. There was nothing for them to gain by lying.

The first time we heard anything out of the norm, we were sitting in the living room one evening with a cup of coffee and listening to one of our favorite Podcasts. The man that was telling about his encounter mentioned seeing some Orbs in the woods earlier that evening. Now we knew what Orbs were from watching Paranormal shows with our daughter. She was all into the Paranormal stuff. She had always loved horror movies. So when the Paranormal shows begin to come on, she watched them all.

This man talked about seeing some small bouncing lights in the woods about half an hour before his encounter. He had been sitting up in his deer stand just scoping things out with his night vision binoculars. He wasn't hunting, so he hadn't brought a gun. He was watching to see what wildlife moved around his area. Once he noticed the orbs moving around, he dropped the night vision and could see them even better with his naked eye. It wasn't long after seeing the orbs that he had his Sasquatch encounter.

Now John and I keep looking over at one another with raised eyebrows, wondering if the other was believing what this witness was saying. The host of the show was his usual polite self and never gave any indication that this story was a little different than most. As usual, after the show, we turned off the computer and discussed what we had just heard.

I had a hard time believing in orbs, even with the paranormal shows I felt like it was just dust or a bug caught on the camera. This man had claimed that they sort of drifted up and down between the trees before they disappeared. That was just hard for me to imagine. John felt the same way I did. But he did have a good point. He said that it is always harder to believe in something you have never seen, just like us seeing the Sasquatch. And we really had no right to question this man's authenticity when we hadn't experienced it ourselves. I wondered if I was supposed to start believing in Fairies now. This was all just a lot to absorb. We agreed that we would keep an open mind as we delved deeper into the world of the Sasquatch. And it would get crazier; I just had no idea at the time.

When we finally got back to check our bag, it was pretty much the same as the one we had left before. The bag had been torn open as had the contents inside. The two apples were gone entirely. The food had been eaten or taken with the wrappers left strewn on the ground.

We carefully examined each wrapper, and there were still not bite marks where anything had chewed them. John quickly headed over to the tree to look for prints. Apparently, the wind had gotten hard a few times as it blew leaves over what he had cleared. There was a small area that looked like it would have been a good print had the leaves not been there. This was frustrating! We were doing everything right, but we weren't getting anything concrete.

John was feeling as frustrated as I was. Here we were freezing our butts off and getting nothing. I knew we couldn't expect activity every time. But at least one tree knock would have made me feel better.

"I think we're going to have to try some night time hunting," John said.

"Excuse me"? "You want us to run around in the woods after dark with a creature that could easily pop our head right off of our shoulders"? I responded, with wide eyes. He could not possibly be thinking this was a good idea. A hundred bad outcomes came to mind in the first thirty seconds. We had no clue what we were doing out here other than what we had learned online. I tried to explain to him that we were the worst type of people to be doing this as usual. He had an explanation that made perfect sense.

"Susan, we are no different from anyone else that has had an encounter. We get out into the woods and try to learn as much as we can. There are no Sasquatch researchers with formal training. We know how to camp, and we know how to hike. Those are the basics. The rest we will figure out as we go".

He did make sense, but it was the "figure it out as we go" part that concerned me. I think we should figure out how to survive an angry Sasquatch before we faced one in the middle of the night. But what did I know?

John was now thinking out loud, and I was becoming more and more concerned.

"We can camp up here, but I'm pretty sure they would want us to stay in the designated camping areas. We would freeze to death in our tent this time of year". I could picture the wheels turning in his mind, and I didn't like it at all.

"I'll figure this out later," he said, picking up his backpack. "Let's get out of this cold." He had finally said something I could agree with. I couldn't get back to the car fast enough. The high today was thirty-four degrees!

Christmas and New Year's came and went with John, and I sticking close to the house. The low temperatures seemed to be locked in place, and there were very few days that it got above freezing. We had read that this was when the Sasquatch seemed to be more active. And if you thought about it, it made perfect sense, there were fewer people outdoors now that the weather was colder, and they could move about more freely.

I knew that this would be our best opportunity to get some good evidence, but I just wasn't too keen on braving these cold temperatures. Now when I was younger, I would not have hesitated to go. But now, it just seemed as if the cold went straight to my bones. I had decided to keep doing my research and not mention anything to John about an outing. I was content to be an "armchair researcher" right on through the winter.

I was content in my warm house until the day John came home with a surprise. He wanted to ride up to the park and talk to the Park Ranger, but he wouldn't tell me why. He said that part would have to be a secret. He told me that he was working on a surprise for me, and the only reason he mentioned it was because he thought that I might enjoy the ride up to the park. He was right that I would appreciate the long drive, but, the part that he wasn't telling me had me a little concerned. I had been married to this man long enough to know when to worry, and now was the time.

I had to promise John that I would only go into the ranger station to get a cup of coffee and I would leave immediately so the two of them could talk in private. I was a bit concerned about this chat that was about to take place. But sticking to my promise was the only way John was going to allow me to go.

When we arrived at the park, the weather was sunny with a slight breeze. The temperature was still just barely above freezing, but the sun helped. I walked with John into the Ranger Station and got my cup of coffee. After I had my coffee in hand, John couldn't get me out the door fast enough. He seemed rather pleased to see that Joe was behind the counter this morning.

I walked back across the parking lot but stopped just before I got to the car. The sun felt good, so I pulled my hood up on my head to stop the wind and walked over to the picnic tables. It would be nice to sit in the sun and enjoy my coffee. I hadn't been sitting there long when I thought I heard a tree knock off in the distance. I immediately pushed my hood off of my head and strained my ears. I was holding my breath waiting for the next sound. The second one caused my heart to leap up in my throat; it was much closer! I turned around to face the direction it came from. I was now staring into the woods with my back to the ranger station.

I heard six knocks while I waited for John to come out! This had my adrenaline going. I regretted not bringing our daypacks with us now. A walk up to the lake might have given us some evidence.

When John came out, he was shocked to see me all excited. I told him what I had heard. There hadn't been any more sounds for about ten minutes. But they had been pretty loud there for a while.

I knew what John was thinking while he stood there looking out into the woods. His next words confirmed my thoughts. "Do you feel like to walking up to the lake"? He asked. I sure did! Hearing those knocks had gotten me all excited.

"Do you think we need to take food with us"? I asked. "I know how crazy this is going to sound. I told him. But the knocks began just as soon as I sat down here. I was wondering if maybe they recognize us as the ones that bring the food." I told him.

John said that it was possible. To stay hidden for so long, they had to be highly intelligent. But there was no way we could know for sure.

We headed up to the lake carrying our coffee cups and a bag filled with Venison Jerkey, Granola Bars, some peanut butter snack crackers and a few cherry pie snack cakes. I felt like we were doing the right thing. We would take the snacks up to the lake and leave them in the usual spot. I had grabbed a pad and pen out of my purse so I could make notes on any changes we found.

The first thing we noticed was that our fallen tree had been moved off of the small path. Upon closer inspection, we could see that it had been pulled off of the trail.
Usually, some kind of small tractor or four wheelers would have been needed to do this, but there were no signs of any equipment being in this area. The other trees were just too close together, they would have had to cut some of the smaller ones to get in here. It appeared to have been done by the Sasquatch, but why?

John and I discussed how strange that was as we walked on toward the lake. There were three new tree structures. Just like the previous ones, these had been made with many different types of tree branches. Most of which had to have been carried from other parts of the woods. John even pointed out that one of them had the long slender leaves of Cat Tails enter woven with some of the branches. These cattails were only found close to the lake.

So we knew that they had been purposely carried here. Still, there was just no proof that a Sasquatch had done this. We could only agree that it would be strange for people to be doing this.

We made it down to the lake and found the bag torn just like it had been the previous times. The only difference was, there were some perfect prints right at the base of the tree! There were two huge prints and a bunch of small ones. They were precisely where John had raked the leaves back. There were still a few leaves there, but you could easily make out the prints.

I was so thrilled to know that it was probably a mother with her young that was getting the food we left. But I was also kicking myself for not having my camera. My cell phone! I instinctively reached into my jacket pocket and remembered leaving it in the car in my purse. John had his flip phone if we needed to call out, so I hadn't bothered to get mine. The camera was a function that I rarely used, and it never crossed my mind. How could I have been so stupid? I explained to John that my phone would have worked, but I had left it back in the car. I could tell that he was considering going back for it. We did need it. But I was afraid it would be dark by the time we got the phone and made it back up here; plus, the fact that neither one of us were in the best shape to do a fast walk to the car and all the way back to the lake, only to have to walk back to the car again.

I knew it was useless. "There is no way we can make it out of here before dark if we go back for the phone," I told him.

John gave me a serious look, If I go back for the phone, I can make it down there and back quicker. If I do a slow jog, I think I could cut the time in half." He said.

"There is no way I am staying here by myself for the next few hours," I told him. And besides, we only have the one phone with us. We don't need to split up".

John wasn't happy about it, but he agreed. And we headed back to the trail with both of us very disappointed. This was a lesson learned. I would keep a bag with a few things we needed in the car at all times.

Chapter 4

A couple of weeks had gone by, and I had forgotten all about the surprise John had been working on. So the afternoon he came home unloading packages caught me completely off guard.

He brought in box after box and stacked them in the middle of the living room floor. To my dismay, they were all boxes from The Bass Pro Shop! What had he gone and done now? I'm looking at all of these boxes and wondering how many hundreds of dollars he had just spent when he looks at me with a huge smile. He looked like a big kid that was thrilled with his great accomplishment. How could I say anything to him? I decided to just bite my lip and give him a chance to explain.

Still smiling, John said, "This would have been here sooner, but I had to order a few of these." I wanted to ask him what "these" were. But instead, I just stood there quietly waiting for him to explain.

"You're going to love this." He said, handing me one of the boxes. I looked at the thick cardboard. "Oh. Here." He said, reaching into his pocket. He pulled out his pocket knife and ran it across the top of the box.

I sat down on the floor by the pile of boxes. As I opened the one on my lap, my fears were now a reality. I pulled out a down filled, double sleeping bag! This could only mean one thing! Cold weather camping! No. No. No. Absolutely not! Freezing at the state park during the day was one thing. I had no intention of needing a sleeping bag. I looked up at John and was just about to tell him exactly how I felt, but he still had that "little boy at Christmas," look on his face as he opened what I assumed to be a tent heater. My heart fell. I was going camping in the cold.

John must have seen the disappointed look on my face because he started to laugh. "Relax," he said. "I pick up the second part to this at five today, and you're going to love it. Now help me open the rest of these boxes". He said. As he cut the top on another box.

Thirty minutes later, I was sitting in the middle of empty boxes and what looked to be enough cold weather camping gear for ten people! Along with two state-of-the-art cell phones and a GPS for each of us. I just knew he had cleaned out the bank account with this purchase. We didn't need all of this stuff. Sure, I enjoyed camping. But I enjoyed it when the weather was hot, and we could go swimming. This right here was nothing short of ridiculous.

I tried to get John to tell me about the other half of the surprise, but he wouldn't tell me anything. At four thirty he got into his truck and left. He would not tell me anything at all, not even where we would be going to use all of this gear. I assumed Alaska. He just kept repeating that he would tell me everything later.

I paced the floor with a cup of coffee in my hand. Every few minutes I would peer through the curtains to see if John had gotten back yet. On one of those many trips by the window, I almost collapsed face first onto the couch. John was backing a camper into the yard. But not just a camper, a HUGE camper. I would later learn that this camper was a forty-two foot, fifth wheel camper. This thing looked like a house on wheels! How had this gotten so out of hand?

I sat down on the couch and waited for John to come in. The sound of the horn from his truck let me know that he expected me to go outside. I reluctantly set my coffee down and put on my coat. I knew that this time I was not going to be able to hide my emotions. This had gone too far. The camper was going back.

An hour later, John and I are sitting at the kitchen counter with coffee and going over a map of the state park. Now I was the one excited! John had explained everything to me. He had gone up to the state park to inquire about camping.

They allowed tents and campers all year. But you could only camp in their designated areas. John planned to take the camper up to the state park and set it up at the camping area. Then, after dark, we would backpack into our research area. We wouldn't be camping there, but we had all of the warm gear to sit up all night if we chose to. Then once we went back to the camper, we had all the comforts of home. I loved this! I even liked the camper after I found out that he had gotten a great deal on a used one. This one had been owned by an elderly couple that only used it twice. It looked brand new!

We looked over the map, marking places along the waterways that we wanted to check out. Our first night-time outing would be close to the habituation area. (I learned this term in a book. It is anywhere you repeatedly leave food or gifts.)

The next morning, we began to pack our things into the camper. We would do some shopping today and head up to the state park tomorrow. We planned to stay a week. That should give us enough time to get some good evidence. I could barely contain my excitement.

During our shopping trip, we realized that you can't just purchase Venison Jerky. We could find everything but Venison. (TIP: After years of trial and error, Venison Jerky works the best and seems to be their favorite. It can only be bought or ordered through Cabela's.)

We decided to buy our Jerky this time at the Ranger Station. But I would order it online from here on out.

We arrived at our camping spot just before lunchtime. I walked beside John and watched as he got our camper set up. Other than ours, there was only one other camper in the camping area. We had seen them as we drove in. Naturally, John and I picked the very last camping spot. The one that was closest to the woods.

I cooked us some lunch, and we ate it at the breakfast nook. This was a small area just across from the kitchen that housed a small table and two benches. It was surrounded by glass. I loved raising the blinds, so we had a fantastic view of the lake and mountains as we ate. I told John that I was utterly in love with our new camper. I was looking forward to sitting right here sometime with a hot cup of coffee and watch the snow fall.

After I cleaned up from Lunch John suggested that we both take a nap since we planned on being up most of the night. He locked our front door, and we both climbed into the queen-sized bed. Now, this was my idea of camping!

I woke to the sound of John flushing the toilet. It was almost dark outside! How had we slept this long? I jumped up from the bed just as John stepped out of the bathroom. "If you will put on some coffee, I will get our gear together," He said.

I was pouring the coffee just as John zipped up the last backpack. We would be hauling more gear than we were used to. But, it was much colder now, we had to be prepared for the weather, and just in case we didn't make it out by daybreak.

We drank our coffee as we waited for the last of the daylight to fade from the sky.

We left the TV and some lights on in the camper. Carefully closing all of the blinds just in case someone came by. John also took the time to put a do not disturb sign on the front door. We shouldered our packs and headed off into the woods. We were lucky that there would be a full moon tonight. That meant that we wouldn't have to use our flashlights very much. We were both wearing new headlamps. But using any kind of light would give us away, so it was best to be as unnoticed as we could; Both for the Sasquatch and the Rangers.

We made it up to our habituation spot and unshouldered our backpacks. I was exhausted! I knew I would eventually get used to the weight. But this first time had almost killed me. We found a spot about ten yards from our tree and sat down in some bushes. I quickly found out that being stealthy had nothing to do with being comfortable. I had dead branches poking me on every part of my body.

Just as I was about to complain to John that we needed to find another area, we heard a tree knock! It was distant. But I liked the confirmation that we weren't alone. Then I began to wonder, did they know we were here?

John and I sat there for a few hours without hearing anything else. We tied our bag of food to the tree and headed back to the camper. My face felt frozen, even under the fleece face mask I was wearing.

Our first week didn't give us much evidence. I captured a few pictures that were questionable, but there was nothing definite.

If we stayed close to the habituation area, the bag would not be touched. But if we left it and moved on up the mountain or went back to the camper, the food would be taken. This got to be very frustrating. John put out two of our new trail cameras to see if we could find out what was taking the food. That didn't work well either. The camera would somehow get bumped and would film the ground or off to one side. Sometimes It wouldn't record anything at all. It would get triggered and be filming, then it would stop for a few seconds. When it started back, the food was already gone. How? Why? This was giving us more questions than answers.

After not getting anything on the trail cameras. John suggested that we leave out a couple of audio recorders close to the area. I figured we had nothing to lose at this point. So we placed them in watertight bags and hung one close to the habituation tree and one close to the first tree structure. We were going to let them record all night and grab them the next morning.

The next morning, I was making us breakfast before we went up to get the recorders and John was using the laptop.

"Come look at this Susan." He said. Pointing to an Article that headlined, "Bigfoot terrorizes family and pets." I read the article over his shoulder. It appeared that a family, (Greg and Pam Reed) were being harassed by a juvenile Sasquatch. It was scaring them to death by throwing rocks at the house at night and making some horrible vocalizations. The local authorities wouldn't do anything and practically called them crazy. That was about the same response they were getting from the people in the group they had posted in. The wife and husband had both seen this Sasquatch and averaged it to be about five or six feet tall. They said there was no mistaking that it was a male. It was reported to be getting into the trash and pulling up the flowers and bushes in the yard. It seemed to be an all-around butthole. I had read stories like this before, and that was the nature of most Juvenile Sasquatch encounters. They acted like adolescent boys for the most part.

'Wow." I said. "I feel sorry for them. That has got to be frightening and annoying at the same time."

'Let's go help them," John said.

'What?" I asked. I was shocked that he even suggested it.

"They are only a few hours up the road. And we are leaving in the morning anyway," John said.

"I don't think we're the right people for this," I said doubtfully. We barely know what we're doing. How in the world can we help someone else"? I questioned.

"We're better than who they have helping them" John added.

I knew he was right. But I didn't feel good about this. How were we supposed to help them? What could we possibly do to make things better?

"OK," I said. "I'll follow your lead," I told him.

Within the hour John had Randy on the phone and had spoken to both him and his wife, Cindy. They claimed that these things were happening almost every night. John got directions. And as luck would have it, they had a large yard for us to park the camper on.

John told them that we would see them tomorrow after lunch. They were thrilled, but I was still skeptical.

We spent most of that day getting our things ready to travel. Everything inside had to be secured, and we had to choose what things we wanted in the truck with us. It was a lot of work. But we were both enjoying it.

Chapter 5

It was late morning before John, and I got on the road. We had chosen to sleep in because we didn't know how busy we would be once we reached the Reed's house.

The drive up the mountain revealed some beautiful scenery. I was really enjoying the trip until John turned the radio on to a ball game. I didn't mind the ball games on the TV. But when he had them on in the car, it drove me nuts.

I promptly dug into my bag and pulled out one of the digital recorders. We hadn't had time to listen to these, and I thought this drive would give me a good start. I plugged in my earphones and settled into my seat.

For a while, I heard nothing but night sounds. A few owls and a couple of airplanes. I could hear a fish or beaver splash in the lake from time to time. And then off in the distance, I heard what sounded like something walking. My heart began to beat a little faster. I could hear the footsteps getting closer to the recorder. I knew this could be any type of wildlife coming down to the lake for a drink. Finally, there was no mistaking that these were bipedal footsteps! I was listening to these footsteps when the recorder began to sound like it was getting banged around pretty good. I could hear it bumping against the tree it was hanging in. There was no wind at all, or I would hear the rustle of the leaves.

It seemed as if something was checking out the recorder. As I Listened, my heart began to beat faster. Something was sniffing the recorder! There was no way of knowing what this was, but it sounded big. When the sniffing stopped, I heard a few deep grunts. Then it seemed like the plastic bag rustling. I couldn't believe I heard this. This had to be the animal that was taking the food! It was messing with the bag now, and I heard it! It sounded like the bag was torn open. I could hear things falling onto the leaves as if the contents of the bag had spilled. There were a few more grunts and then the crinkling of what seemed to be the Venison Jerky package! Listening to this was amazing! I wished we had left a trail camera out. We were missing what could have been some good shots. Then I remembered how the trail came experiment had gone. Why could we catch such excellent audio but nothing on the trail cameras? Could these things tell the difference? While I was contemplating this, the animal near the recorder let out an ear-splitting whoop! I jumped causing my knee to hit the dash.

John looked over at me with raised eyebrows. Before I could explain to him what I was listening too. The loud whoop I had heard was immediately answered by another one that sounded to be on the other side of the lake. I had read about the whoop sound they made, but I had never experienced it. Hearing it so clearly actually gave me chills. Just like what I had read, I agreed that this had to be some sort of communication.

I wondered if they were telling one another that the food was there? Why else would they be communicating now? I turned off the recorder as John pulled into a gas station.

John said that he had heard on the radio that some snow was expected today on up the mountain. He wanted to fill the trucks reserve tank and the two reserve tanks in the camper. If we did happen to get snowed-in, we would have plenty of fuel for the camper. I loved the way that John was always thinking ahead and protecting us. It had been one of the qualities that caused me to marry him.

After fueling up and grabbing snacks, we were back on the road. I rewound my recorder and let John listen to it. He was as fascinated as I was. We knew we would keep this to ourselves. There was just really no way to prove audio. Maybe the Sasquatch knew this? Is that why we could get perfect audio and no video?

I plugged my recorder into the truck's radio via USB port. We listened to the audio until we found the road that would lead us to the Reed's house.

We had turned off the main road about an hour back, where we had come through a small town. We were out in the country now, and it was looking like a good place for some Sasquatch to be. They could be easily hidden out here.

The road the Reed's lived on wasn't paved. And I worried about the camper. John patted my leg and told me to relax. The woods came right up to the road, and they were every bit as thick as the ones at the state park. Occasionally, there would be an opening where you could see a reasonable distance through the trees. We were passing one of these openings when I asked John to stop. About thirty yards from the truck was a perfect arch. We knew now, the Sasquatch was here.

I was about to give up hope of anyone living this far out when we drove around a bend that opened up to a huge yard. There was a two-story farmhouse entirely surrounded by woods. A small stream cut a path through the side yard on the left. It was rustically beautiful here. An old outhouse stood off to the right side of the house near the woods. You could tell by the weathered wood that this was from a much simpler time. There was more than enough space in their huge yard for our camper.

A young man and woman came out onto the front porch smiling. Both raised their arm to wave at us. I assumed this was Randy and Cindy Reed. Randy was tall and skinny with short brown hair. His winter coat seemed to be swallowing his slender body.

Cindy was much shorter with red curly hair that she had pulled back into a ponytail. Her thick hair looked as if it were straining to get loose and hang in wild curls around her face. She stood there smiling, with her arms crossed against the cold.

The man bounded down the front steps and started toward the truck as John let his window down. When he approached us, I was comforted by his warm smile. He reached his right hand through the open window to shake Johns. "I'm Randy Reed sir," He said. "Thank you for coming." "Hi mam," He said glancing over to me. Cindy slowly made her way over to join Randy at the truck. After all the introductions were over, John asked Randy where we should park. Randy's response was "anywhere that we felt comfortable." I already liked this young couple.

Randy helped John get our camper set up while Cindy and I watched from the porch. The wind had died down some, but light snow had begun to fall. When the men finished, Cindy invited us all in for coffee.

The kitchen was huge with a roaring fireplace. I hadn't seen a house like this since I was a kid. I was immediately in love with the place.

For the next few hours, we sat around the big kitchen table drinking coffee and enjoying some of Cindy's homemade cinnamon rolls while they told us what had been going on.

The activity seemed to have started last spring when Randy noticed the stream through the yard had almost stopped running. He followed the stream down through the woods and found a place where it had been damned up causing the water in the nearby swamp to flood. He undammed the area and went back home. He used this water for his garden, and he was just starting to plant. He assumed the damn had been caused by beavers and never thought about it again. Two nights later. He heard what he thought was kids throwing rocks against the side of the house. He grabbed his gun and went out on the porch to scare them off.

As he walked to the edge of the porch, he heard a growl that made his blood run cold. Even with the shotgun in his hands, he hurried back inside. He didn't tell Cindy what had happened. He didn't want to upset her. The next day, he found numerous rocks near the side of the house. They had come from the stream. He assumed that kids had thrown the stones. But he couldn't explain the growl he had heard. He pushed it to the back of his mind and tried to forget about it.

The rocks continued to hit the side of the house a few nights a week. Randy finally got fed up with it and decided to sit out and wait on the vandals. That night as he sat behind the house and waited, he saw this thing walk out of the woods and up to the side of the house. It stopped and turned its head as if to sniff the wind. It then looked directly at Randy and let out a scream that hurt his ears. It turned and hurried back into the woods the same way it had come out. Randy ran into the house not looking back. He knew he had just seen a bigfoot. (Randy and Cindy use the term Bigfoot, which is fine. I just prefer the name Sasquatch when referring to these creatures.)

After this encounter, Randy and Cindy both had seen it occasionally, just at the edge of the woods during the day, as if it were watching them. At night, it would steal produce, pull up Cindy's flowers and knock over garbage cans. The Reed's also had two small dogs that would run out into the woods barking. Cindy feared for her little dogs, so Randy had built a fence just out the back door. They would only let the dogs out into the fence when one of them could watch them. This was no way for this young couple to have to live. I wanted to help them. I wasn't sure what we could do. But I wanted to try.

John and I excused ourselves to the camper. We had to come up with a game plan. We decided to take a walk out in the woods and get a feel for the property while it was still daylight. Then we would wait in the camper tonight to see if anything happened. I wasn't too crazy about being out in some strange woods at night. I wanted to see it first during the day.

John and I grabbed the recorders, fixed up one of our treat bags and with the camera, we were ready to go. We walked along the stream as we headed into the woods. The snow had gotten a little harder, but not much of it was sticking to the ground.

John tied off branches so we could easily find our way back. We found arches and structures on our walk and a couple of prints, but they weren't clear enough to cast. We didn't have any doubt that Sasquatch frequented this area. I snapped photos to show Randy and Cindy. We found a place on the stream that looked to be where Randy had done the clearing. We tied up the treat bag and hung our recorders.

It was time to go back to the camper now and wait. As we turned to go, we heard a single tree knock off in the distance. I don't know why I did this, but I turned back around and yelled out, "Stop scaring these nice people! If you want to stay here, you have to stop scaring them!" John looked at me with a raised eyebrow, indicating that I had just lost my mind.

To this day, I don't know what made me do that, all I know is that it just felt right. We slowly walked back to the camper removing the ties as we went.

Randy and Cindy invited us to dinner that night. The only way I would go is for them to promise to have dinner with us the next night. We all agreed, so John and I left the camper about seven to walk over to the house.

Cindy was an excellent cook, and our dinner had been fantastic. We lingered over coffee chatting like old friends. I had started to get tired and was ready to go back to our camper. We had just had a long day, and I was beginning to feel worn out. John and I said goodnight and started back across the yard. Randy stood on the porch as if to watch over us as we walked home.

John had left the front light on at our camper door so it would be easier to see the steps. Just as I was about to step up onto the bottom rung. John said, "Wait a minute." He bent down and picked up something shiny off the top step. I couldn't tell what it was. I had just seen the light glisten off of it when he picked it up.

"What was that?" I asked. "Go on in," John said, as he turned and waved at Randy. Following me into the camper. John closed the door turning off the outside light. Then he held out his hand to reveal a Granola wrapper. It was the same type we had left out in the woods! How in the world had it gotten onto our steps?

I was stunned. "How did this get here"? I asked.

"I'm not sure," John said. "I'm as stumped as you are." Unfortunately, we had to look at all possibilities. This included the Reed's. We didn't know them well enough so we couldn't rule out the possibility of a hoax. I hated to even think that way. But we had to. The wrapper was the same as we had found them before. There were no teeth marks. It had been torn open.

The snow had stopped overnight and the next morning was beautifully sunny. There were small patches of snow remaining, but I was sure it would be gone by noon. John and I would be heading back out to the woods this morning. We would check the bag and have a look around. Tonight, we would be out and waiting for anything to show up.

I cleaned up from breakfast while John readied our gear. I was still thinking about the wrapper as we headed off into the woods.

I had read about the Sasquatch leaving small gifts. But this one here was supposed to be acting up. Why would it decide to leave something now? And why leave it at our camper? I could only hope to one day find the answers to my million questions.

Once again John tied off the trees as we made our way through the woods. It didn't take us long this time to find the treat bag. It was about forty yards up the stream. Just like the others, it had been torn down with the side ripped out of it. We continued on to see if we could find the remaining wrappers. The wrappers lay at the base of the tree. Well, most of the wrappers were there. A few of them were missing. We looked around the area and didn't find them. We had no way of knowing what had taken them. There were two Granola and one Jerky wrapper missing. The others were strewn around the area. We picked up all the paper to be more closely examined later.

We gathered the two recorders, and John left two trail cameras. But this time, we made sure to camouflage the two cameras. No one would know they were there. If a person were messing around with our bag, we would have them on camera tomorrow.

We walked around the woods for the next couple of hours. Closely examining tree structures and arches. I was taking pictures and writing down notes. John had decided it was best to go back to the camper now and go over our evidence, then we could get some rest before our nighttime investigation. Just as I started to turn around John grabbed my arm and pointed. About thirty yards down a ravine, something was walking. Through the trees, it appeared to be a cinnamon color. From where we were standing, there was no way to know exactly what this was. Judging by the height, I would say that this was a juvenile or female Sasquatch; yet I couldn't completely rule out a bear until I heard the noise. The sound was faint because of the distance, but you could hear whatever this was making noises as it walked. "Warble, warble, Bloosh, warble" The "bloosh," sound it was making sounded like rocks being thrown into the water, but there was no water near us. Then the warble sounded like a person that couldn't talk correctly trying to say marble. I stood there fascinated with what we were experiencing. It was making these sounds almost as a human would mumble under their breath. My heart was pounding in my chest, and I was frozen in place! We were only catching glimpses of this creature's fur as it moved between the trees and underbrush. I couldn't explain what this was. The only rational thing that came to mind was that an unsuspecting juvenile Sasquatch was walking through the woods not expecting us to be there. I ever so slowly raised my camera. Just as I got this thing sighted in my lens. It was gone! Just that quickly. Gone.

John and I stood there a few more minutes with neither of us speaking.

"Where in the hell did it go"? John asked in a whisper.

"It seems to have just disappeared" I answered.

"But it was right there," John replied.

Yes, it had been right there. But it wasn't now. The only thing that made sense was that it had moved further up the ravine into the trees where we could no longer see it. That's what my mind was telling me anyway. Just then we heard a tree crash to the ground. The sound had come from the ravine. Now I have no way of knowing if this tree just fell of its own accord or if it was pushed over. Just having a random tree fall at this exact moment would be one strange coincidence. It was deafening. John took my hand. "That's our sign to leave." He said softly. We turned around and slowly made our way back to the camper. We didn't know enough about these creatures to know if this was a territorial display or a sign of aggression. And to be honest, it could have been a coincidence. But for safety reasons, we left the area.

We spent most of our day going over evidence, then I cooked an early dinner for us and the Reed's. They were both amazed when they came into our camper. I don't think they were expecting it to be so roomy. And the fireplace blew Randy's mind. Of course, the fire was really just a heater. But it looked real with our TV hanging above it.

After John gave them the grand tour, we all sat down to eat. Cindy loved our breakfast nook as much as I did. I had raised all of the blinds so we could enjoy a view of the surrounding woods.

I had just sat back down after pouring coffee when Randy handed something to John. "This was on our front steps this morning," he said. John examined a Venison Jerky wrapper and then looked up at me. "This was ours," he said. We then had to explain to Cindy and Randy about the treat bag we hang up. Neither of us mentioned the Granola wrapper.

At first, Randy was concerned with the fact that we were feeding them. He had read online about the bad parts of habituation. We explained to him the difference in our treat bag and habituation. Our treat bag was just a simple way to find out if any were in the area. And a way to let them know that we weren't there to harm them.

The Jerky wrapper had been torn from the bottom, and there were no chew marks on it. Randy seemed fascinated when we told him that is how all of our treat wrappers looked. He said that it was strange to him that a smaller animal hadn't come along and smelled the food then chewed on the already empty wrapper. John and I had thought about this too. Our only conclusion was that the smaller animals were frightened away by the smell of an apex predator. Why else would they not attempt to chew the empty wrappers?

Randy told us that he had found random feathers and small stones around the house since all of this had been going on, but he had never put two and two together until this morning when he found the wrapper on his front porch step. Cindy said it scared her just to know that this thing was walking around the yard at night. I tried to get Cindy to see this sasquatch as a young teenage boy that was bored and getting into mischief. He hadn't attempted to harm anyone; he had only scared them. We all fear what we don't understand. Cindy reluctantly agreed with me.

I went into the bedroom and came back with a small sandwich bag for Cindy. Inside the bag, I had placed a few marbles, a few colored beads, and a few colored stones. I told her to leave some of these out tonight in the exact spot that Randy had found the wrapper and see what happened.

Randy and Cindy thanked us for dinner and John walked home with them. Cindy was uneasy about being outside after dark, so John and Randy both carried shotguns on their walk up to the house. I cleaned up the kitchen wondering what our night would hold.

After dark, John and I positioned ourselves at the edge of the woods to where we could see the side of the Reed's house and their front porch. If anything came up to the house, we would see it.

John and I had been outside for a few hours, and things had been quiet. I was thankful now for all of the winter gear John had bought. I had to admit that I was actually warm. But now that I was warm, the hard part would be staying awake.

John and I were sitting on the ground with our backs against two trees. We were passing the FLIR camera back and forth to keep an eye on the surrounding woods. John had the parabolic mic to his ear when he reached over and touched my hand. I looked at him just as he put his finger to his lips signaling me to be quiet. He had heard something. He pointed in the direction the sound was coming from, but I wasn't picking up anything on the FLIR. I sat anxiously waiting for something to happen.

After about five minutes John removed the headphones and said that he had heard something Bi-pedal approaching, but it suddenly stopped. It stood there for a few minutes, making a low grunting noise then it turned and walked away. He thought that we may have just been detected. If that was the case, I knew there would be no more activity tonight. We agreed to sit out a little longer and see what happened.

My watch said it was nearing two in the morning and I had given up for the night. I was about to tell John when I heard something falling through the branches of the tree I was leaning on. John and I both looked up just as something else came tumbling through the branches. This time John was hit on the shoulder. He felt around on the ground to find what he had just been hit with and we were both shocked to see a small smooth river stone!

I was about to stand up when John grabbed my hand. He leaned over and whispered. "Don't move. Let's just see what happens."

Was this man nuts? Did he seriously think it was a good idea to sit here in the dark and get hit by rocks from a Sasquatch? It didn't make good sense to me. I know the stones were small and didn't hurt us, but that could quickly change. I also didn't like the fact of one of these creatures being behind me in the dark.

I was not comfortable at all, and my fight or flight was just about to kick in. Once that happened, it was every man for himself. I didn't feel good about it, but I did as John asked and settled back onto my butt. I took a deep breath and tried to relax.

What happened next will haunt me for the rest of my life. Those small stones had been a warning that we didn't heed. I heard the crack then a loud creaking John, and I didn't have time to react before the tree was pushed down on top of us! Luckily the ones we were leaning against took most of the weight, but we were still covered with branches from the top of the tree. We struggled to our feet and made a hasty retreat to the camper leaving our gear buried beneath the tree.

Inside the camper, I still didn't feel safe. My heart was still pounding, and I couldn't wrap my head around what had just happened. Had this thing tried to kill us? But why?

John didn't think it had intentionally tried to hurt us, he saw it as a scare tactic. (It worked and it worked well.) He believes that because the rocks didn't scare us away that it had to try something different.

I went to bed that night wondering how in the world we were going to help this young couple. John and I had only planned to be here for a few days. This could take weeks or even months. We had to find an answer and soon.

The next morning, the Reeds let us know that the things they had left on the front porch were gone and in their place was a crow's feather. It suddenly made sense to me! This Sasquatch wanted us out of the way so it could get to the front porch without being seen. We had just been in its way, and it had tried to get us to move. Now I'm thinking that we aren't the smartest species on the planet.

I had an idea. I wasn't sure if this was going to work or not, but I had to try. Randy had some huge logs where he had cut up an old tree. I asked him if he and John could move one of those logs to the tree line on the back side of the house. They humored me and rolled the log just as I had asked. Then I had a couple of favors to ask Cindy. I wanted a small stuffed animal and some fake flowers. She was able to find everything I asked for.

That evening, just before sunset I walked down to the log that they had stood on end for me. (It resembled a stump now.) I placed the stuffed bear, fake flowers and a few colored stones on the stump. I walked about five feet away and hung up a recorder. John and I would stay in the camper tonight.

The next morning, all of my gifts were gone. There was nothing left in their place, but beside the stump was the most perfect footprint I had ever seen! That was my gift. John and I cast the print, and that was my gift from the Sasquatch.

It would be the first of many prints. But it's the one that I hold dear.

We stayed a few more days with the Reed's, A week in total. And things seemed to have quietened down. I told them that if and when it picked back up to try leaving a few gifts out. Nothing edible, but to leave colorful and shiny objects. This was three years ago, and it is still working for them. When they hear a howl at night or the house gets hit. They take a few objects out to the stump, and things get quiet again. Cindy has even been giving them cut fresh flowers since they no longer pull them up. I think this juvenile, like any other child, had gotten bored. These gift objects seemed to make it happy.

Chapter 6

I guess you could say that John and I had been bitten by the "Bigfoot bug." If we were spending time at home, we couldn't wait to get back out there. Our families and close friends thought we were nuts. And maybe we were. But we were enjoying every minute of this.

We spent time at different parks in different states. We captured some pretty cool evidence, and we were learning a lot. If we saw an interesting encounter online, we could pack up the camper and head that way. It was really awesome to be able to do this. We met a lot of nice people. Some we were able to help, but others left us scratching our heads. These creatures were never predictable. But we learned something new each time we went out.

After the first year, John and I upgraded our camper to a newer model with a lot of bells and whistles. We were spending more time in it than at home anyway. Our new one had a larger kitchen and bathroom. And we were able to set up our own research area in the living room with two full-sized computers, a large map, and fully equipped desks.

John and I have had a lot of adventures, and there are many stories we could tell you. But I'm just giving you the ones that stuck out in our minds as being the most significant.

A year or so, after getting our new camper, we were sitting at home one night. John was online while I was curled up on the couch with a book. I had just gotten over a horrible cold, (It felt like the flu.) And I hadn't gained all of my strength back yet. So the couch and a warm blanket was the perfect place for me.

John was reading about recent encounters, and he found one that interested him. Numerous witnesses had spotted a large male Sasquatch on a stretch of road north of us. This Sasquatch had been seen ten plus times in the last six months, and there were reports of local farmers having problems with missing livestock and produce. A few researchers had already followed up on this. But none of them were able to help. In our years of research, I had come to realize that most of the researchers showed up at a location for the evidence they could collect. Very few of them were actually there to help the people that were being harassed. I'm not exactly sure why I could only speculate that they weren't sure how to help other than killing the Sasquatch. I can half-way understand this. But didn't they owe it to the people to at least try to help?

I knew that John was ready to go. But in my weakened state, I just wasn't feeling it. I wanted to be home when I was sick. (Don't we all?)

Naturally, John assured me that I could spend this trip in the camper. He would handle everything on his own. I thought about it and figured that it wouldn't be too bad as long as I stayed in the camper. Spring had just started, and the air was still a little chilly. I didn't need to be running around outside just yet. Especially up in the mountains. I reluctantly agreed to go.

John would do some further research and see what witnesses he could contact. If we could reach out to the witnesses, this always made it easier for us. We could get a first-hand account of what they had experienced and find a place locally to park the camper. Upon meeting the witness, we could tell within the first hour if they had actually seen a Sasquatch or maybe it was a case of mistaken identity. I don't like to call anyone that has had an experience a hoaxer. I wasn't there to see what they saw, so I have no idea of what experience they had or didn't have. It is not my place to Judge.

It took John a couple of days to get in touch with a farmer by the name of Tom Partain. Tom and his wife Lily had seen this Sasquatch on the road below their farm twice. And he thought it might be what was taking his chickens. As luck would have it, Tom owned some pasture land just down the road from his house. He said he would be happy to remove a section of fence so we could park the camper there. We were packing up to leave the next morning.

Knowing that I had been sick and still wasn't feeling all that good. John cut me some slack on this trip. When it came time to eat, he would drive into the parking lot of a restaurant and pull into the back where he would park the camper and go in for our food. He would bring it back out, and we would eat in the camper.

The first night on the road, we parked in a Wal-Mart parking lot. It was already getting pretty late, but this Wal-Mart was open 24/7 so John went in. He came back out pushing a cart full of groceries that I could just heat in the microwave. Along with two boxes of hot tea for me, a beautiful fleece throw blanket and two paperback books. I was laughing as he unloaded all of his shopping treasures. This was indeed an extraordinary man.

We took our time traveling up the mountain. The scenery was just, and I had John pull over a few times just so I could snap some pictures.

On day three, just after lunchtime, we pulled into another Wal-Mart parking lot. John fished his cell phone out of his pocket and called Mr. Partain. He was going to meet us here and then we would follow him out to his house.

About twenty minutes later an older model pickup truck pulled in beside us. The man that got out was short and slim. He looked to be about seventy, I could tell right away that he was a farmer. He wore the usual scuffed cowboy boots with jeans and a flannel shirt. His cowboy hat covered his thinning gray hair. And his smile was warm and friendly. He didn't hesitate to walk up to John and offer his hand. Then he removed the cowboy hat and spoke to me. "How ya doin mam"? He said. I liked him already.

Mrs. Partain got out of the truck and walked over to us. Unlike her husband, she wore a heavy buckskin coat over her jeans and shirt. Her cowboy boots were scuffed and worn. You could tell that they were used to a lot of outdoor work. She too had a smile that could light up a room and was not too far below her husband in age.

After the introductions, John asked if they would like to go somewhere to get coffee so we could talk. Mrs. Partain. (Lily) Wouldn't hear of it. She had baked a cake for us and said it wouldn't take but a minute to make coffee.

Tom told us that he would stop on the bridge where the Sasquatch had been seen and then he would take us on up to the pasture where we could get settled in. We followed the old pick up out of the parking lot and out of town.

As we drove out into the countryside, we were surrounded by woods and rolling hills. It was amazingly beautiful. I could understand why a Sasquatch would want to live here. The landscape went on for miles without a house in sight.

We turned onto quite a few secondary roads. I now realized why Tom had insisted on driving us in. He had said that the GPS sometimes didn't give accurate directions on these little backroads. I just hoped that John would be able to find his way out of here. I was completely lost.

The roads we were on now, were small and entirely surrounded by woods. There were a few houses, but they were set very far apart. In other words, your neighbors weren't within walking distance. You would have to drive over to see them. Each time we met an oncoming car, John would have to slow down and get as far off the road as he could to let them pass. This resulted in tree branches scraping the truck and the camper causing some terrible noises. I could see John physically draw up each time this happened. I just knew he was thinking about the cash he was going to have to lay out for a new paint job.

Tom finally tapped his breaks before stopping, letting John know that we were coming up on the bridge. We pulled off to the side of the road, and got out of our vehicles. Tom showed us exactly where the Sasquatch had been when they had seen it. It had been standing just at the side of the bridge. It never crossed the road. It just stood beside the bridge for a moment before turning and going back down the bank.

I knew what John was going to do, so I followed. We made our way down the bank underneath the bridge. There had to be something that was causing the Sasquatch to come to this area. And John was going to see if there were any signs. With spring just getting started the trees and underbrush were putting out green leaves. This meant that the briars were already coming back with a vengeance. And there were plenty of them on the bank between the road and the water down below.

John and I slowly made our way down to the bottom. I could see why it was so easy for the Sasquatch to turn and disappear. This was a really steep bank. With two steps it would have been low enough to not be seen from the road.

It was really muddy under the bridge. There were a few spots that looked like it may have been footprints at one point. But they had deteriorated with the weather. It didn't take but a minute for John to find a reason why the Sasquatch frequented this bridge.

From where we stood I could see, Red Mulberry bushes, Red Elderberry bushes, Wild Strawberry plants, Blueberry bushes, Blackberry bushes, Service Berry bushes, Persimmon, and Crab Apple trees. This was a smorgasbord for any animal. I'm sure it also drew in the deer, and other wildlife and these too would make a potential meal for a Sasquatch. It made perfect sense that the Sasquatch had been seen here. John gave me a knowing smile as we climbed back up the bank.

"I think we may found part of the problem," John told Tom. There is an abundant food source just under this bridge. Tom was shocked, but in agreement with us that it would definitely attract them. We loaded back into the trucks and drove on out to Tom's property.

Tom turned off the road and into a pasture between the trees. This was going to be our home for the next few days. The pasture was pretty big. It looked to be about twenty acres of tall grass that was completely closed in by woods. John drove us into the field and turned around so the truck would be facing out.

I stayed in the warm truck as John set up our camper. Tom had told us that when we were ready, that they were the very next driveway on the right. He and Lily left us to get settled in.

I was tired and really wanting a nap, but we had promised the Partain's to come over for cake and coffee. I had considered sending John by himself, but I thought that would be rude, so I reluctantly went with him.

The Partain's had a beautiful brick house that was set back off the road. On one side they had land plowed for a massive garden and on the other side of the house, was fencing for what looked to be, horses, goats and maybe a few cows. I could see the chicken house set back further in the yard with a fence around it. It was the closest to the woods.

As we drove into the yard, Tom came out on the porch to greet us. I could smell something wonderful wafting from the inside of the house. The smell made my stomach growl. It was then that I realized we had missed lunch. Maybe coming wasn't such a bad idea.

Lily had made homemade biscuits with Venison steak in case we were hungry. And she had a pound cake with some of her homemade jellies to go with it. The food was terrific as I was starving. While we ate, Tom told us about what had been going on for the past year at their place.

It had all began with his deer stand being ripped down from a tree. Tom said that he liked to get a couple of deer and a few turkeys every year to fill his freezer. It had all began with his deer stand being ripped down from a tree. Tom said that he liked to get a couple of deer and a few turkeys every year to fill his freezer. He had never had any problem hunting out here on his own land. But last year, his deer stand was torn down. He just assumed some random kids had done it, so he put it back up. Within the week it was torn down again, and this time, the metal on it was bent beyond repair. He looked around for four-wheeler tracks, knowing it took more than human strength to do this. There were no signs of anyone having been there.

Now that he didn't have a deer stand he was having to spend his time in the woods sitting on the ground. He said that it was harder to hunt due to your scent carrying on the wind. And for some reason, he had felt strangely vulnerable on the ground.

He had been out hunting about two hours when he heard a scream like he had never heard before. He said it made the hair on the back of his neck stand up and all he could think of was getting out of those woods. He knew that something wasn't right and he didn't want to see what had made that noise. He didn't mention this to Lily.

He didn't go back out in the woods for the next few weeks. He intended to wait until he could get another tree stand. He had no idea if that strange animal was still out there or not and he wasn't taking any chances. He would feel much better in the woods if he were thirty or forty feet up.

One evening about five thirty, he and Lily decided to go to the local sporting goods store where he could price the deer stands. The sun was just beginning to set as he drove onto the road and headed toward the old bridge.

Nearing the bridge his eyes had begun to register something strange standing just off the road. By the time he realized this wasn't a tree, Lily had let out a scream causing him to hit the brakes hard. He came to a sudden stop, staring at this "thing" while it stared back at them. He described this Sasquatch to be about nine feet tall. It was covered in dirty black hair. The black hair is what had caused Tom to think earlier it had just been the shadow of a tree. He said this thing was absolutely huge and very muscular. I could tell that the size of this thing had really frightened him. As he was describing it to us, he repeated more than once that the chest on this thing was just unbelievable and the muscles in the arms and legs let him know that it could rip the truck apart if it wanted to. He told us that there was no mistaking this thing was a male. It had turned to look straight at the truck before stepping back down the bank and disappearing.

He sat there just a moment trying to gain his senses back before he quickly drove over the bridge. Once past the bridge, he realized that he had been holding his breath and Lily had been screaming for him to "Go!" the whole time.

While Tom talked, reliving this encounter, I could tell that it had deeply bothered him. Once Tom was finished telling us about first seeing the Sasquatch. I did something I had never done before. I turned to Lily and asked her to tell us what she saw. I wanted to hear her experience too.

Lily basically told us what Tom had said, but I felt like she had more to say. I reached across the table and took her hand. I looked right into her eyes when I said, "I have seen them too, and we're here to help." Her eyes immediately went to Tom and then quickly back to me. That was my sign that there was more to this story! I just had to be gentle with them now and try to gain their trust.

John told Tom, "We're not here for the evidence. We know that these creatures exist. We came here to try to help you guys out and to further our own research, but we have to know the whole story. We promise it will never go any further than this room unless you say otherwise".

Tom looked over at Lily and nodded his head. Lily looked at me saying, "This was our first time seeing it. But it wasn't the only time.

The next time we saw it, Tom and I were out working in the garden. We had produce that had recently gone missing, and we were trying to gather it all every day and take it into the house. We thought that maybe some kids had been messing around. We had seen some small bare footprints in the dirt that could have only come from kids. While we were working, I had stopped to stretch my back. When I looked up across the far pasture, I saw a black bear come out of the tree line. I told Tom to look, and we watched it walk about twenty yards from the tree line. Then it just stood up on its hind legs, turned and walked back into the woods! Tom and I both were shocked. I couldn't believe what I had just seen. Tom said, "Lily, I think it's time we go inside." At first, I didn't know what he meant, but then I remembered that thing by the bridge and I got really scared. A few nights later, we were watching TV after dinner when the chickens started having a fit. Tom grabbed his gun and went out the kitchen door. I was scared that thing would be out there, so I stood in the doorway and watched. I could see Tom's flashlight as he went across the yard. The light showed around the chicken coop a little, and then it went toward the woods. That's when I saw this thing just at the edge of the trees in the backyard! Toms light lit it up. It stood there for just a second and then it opened its mouth real big and let out a yell that I will never forget. I guess it was more like a roar than a yell. It was deafening. It yelled at us and then just turned and disappeared into the woods. That was the beginning of our missing chickens.

It took two that night, then other nights it would get two and sometimes three".

I gave her a few moments to see if she was going to say anything else. I asked if these were the only times they had seen it. Lily looked over at Tom, and he said, "No, we have seen it a few other times. More times than I ever wanted to". He added. I waited patiently for him to continue.

Lily and I were coming home from Church one Sunday evening, as we pulled into the driveway, we saw that thing on the far side of the pasture walking down on all fours again. It looked just like a big bear, but we both knew it wasn't. We sat there in the car watching this thing. It walked about twenty yards out of the tree line and stopped. Then a smaller one came out of the trees. It walked almost up to the big one, but then it turned and ran back to the woods. And when I say, ran. I mean this thing moved at an unnatural speed. It flew across that pasture. The big one stayed still for just a moment and then it moved on off into the trees. Lily and I got out of the car and hurried into the house. You just don't feel safe being outside when you know those things are so close.

I knew that the Sasquatch was seeing this as a secure food source. I wondered just what we could do to get them to move on.

Tom let out a long sigh and continued. "It was bad enough to see them across the pasture and have them stealing our chickens. But when they got brave enough to come up to the house and start going through the garbage I had enough. I got angry when I had to start picking up trash that was strewn all over the yard every day. I got my gun out and went looking for it. I figured if I could shoot it then our problems would be over. Lily begged me not to, she was scared I would get hurt trying to kill this thing. But I was angry and hot-headed, so I went off looking for it. I hadn't been out in the woods very long when I came across our neighbor sitting down near the fence line with his own shotgun. We talked for a few minutes, and I finally got up the nerve to ask him if he had seen anything strange. He looked relieved and told me that he was out there looking for this thing too. It had taken a whole litter of his hunting dogs pups. It had been coming to his place to messing things up. So he crossed the fence, and we went looking for this thing together. This was when he told me that it had some young. He had seen a smaller one with it and two littles". I stopped him right there. "This Sasquatch has a family"? I asked. Now it was my turn to exchange a glance with John.

Tom took a sip of his coffee and continued. "I knew it had what I assumed to be a mate. But I didn't know anything about the little 'uns until that day. After a few hours of walking, we finally came out of the woods onto the swamp in the far back end of both our properties.

We were making our way through this swamp when we heard a whistle. Both of us stopped. This whistle had sounded like it came from a human. That is when Ray saw the hair through the trees. He pointed in the direction, and I could see it. Slowly walking through the trees. But this one was a dark brown color. It wasn't black like the one I had seen before. This wasn't big enough to be the male. This one only looked to be about five or six feet tall. We stood there and watched her for about two minutes. She broke the tree line and walked out of the trees on the edge of the swamp. She was about forty yards away from us. She walked down to the edge of the water and knelt down. This thing began to drink water from its hand just like a human would do. That is when the two little ones came out of the underbrush. One of them walked down to where she was at the water, but the other stayed just inside the tree line. It never crossed my mind to shoot. I couldn't have. This was a mother with young. I don't care what kind of animal it is; you just don't do that. We stood there watching this mother and young one have a drink when the other young one looked up and saw us. He let out a screech that sounded a lot like a barred owl. But it was louder and deeper. In the seconds it took for this thing to scream. The mother grabbed the other one and was gone into the trees in a flash. By the time my mind registered what was happening a deafening howl came from behind us! Ray and I spun around and there, not twenty feet from us stood that big black male! I don't know if Ray meant to or if it was just a reflex, but his gone went off hitting this thing in the arm.

It let out a yell that almost busted my ears! I have never in my life experienced anything this loud. Just as soon as this thing yelled, the female screamed from the woods! It only took a second for Ray to throw down his gun and turn to run. I saw Ray take off and I can tell you, I wasn't far behind him. We were both splashing through that swamp running for our lives! Now I'm getting on in years, and it didn't take me long to be out of breath, and I knew I had to stop. Plus, the fact that running with a loaded gun was both awkward and downright dangerous. I slowed down to a light jog trying my best to keep moving. Ray was up ahead of me, and when I fell back, he slowed down. I guess he was going to turn around to see where I was, but the minute he turned his eyes went wider than I have ever seen a person do and the next thing I knew was something hit me across the back really hard, and I was then flying through the air. I can remember seeing Ray all wide-eyed and slack-jawed as I flew through the air toward him. Hours later, I woke up here at the house in my own bed. Lily and Ray were sitting at the kitchen table having coffee when I got up. My head and left knee were throbbing, all of my muscles were sore and aching. But other than that I felt all right. Lily informed me that Ray had run all the way to his house and got his truck. He drove that old truck like a bat out of hell through the pastures getting back to me. He had even run over some of his own fence lines to get to me. He loaded me up in his truck and brought me home". Tom took another sip from his cup. "Things just got worse from that day on," he said.

I was speechless. I couldn't believe what I was hearing. We had come to try to help these people. But now we had a large, angry male Sasquatch that was hell-bent on sticking around. What had we gotten ourselves in to?

Tom went on to tell us that over the next few months, it stole ten goats, three pigs, numerous chickens, and six cows. It would either kill them in the pen and leave a blood trail, or it would take the whole animal not leaving anything but big footprints behind.

I looked over at John, and I could tell that he was as fascinated as I was. By now, we had dealt with a few Sasquatch that was said to be aggressive. But we had never dealt with anything on this scale before. This could be deadly if we didn't handle it just right. I have to admit that I was downright frightened now. I couldn't let the Partain's know how I felt, but I was ready to pack up and leave.

When John and I got back to the camper that night, he drove the truck right up to the front door. We had forgotten to leave the light on, and it was dark. For the first time, I wondered about our safety in the camper.

John and I sat up a long time that night discussing what we should do. Basically, anything we did ran a chance of us only making this thing angrier. That was not what we wanted for the Partain's or us. We would have to come up with a plan. I went to sleep that night wondering if it were watching our camper.

I got my answer early the next morning. When John and I left the camper to walk the woods, we saw Huge footprints all around the trailer. It looked as if it had come to see what this was.

The woods and pasture were full of Sasquatch signs, Tree structures, arches, footprints, bent fencing, broken limbs, and trees. All the things that we would look for with a reported sighting. But this time, we didn't have to look hard to find them, they were everywhere! Apparently, this creature had been here a lot longer than the Partain's thought, and It wasn't one just moving through. This one had lived here for a while. John and I hadn't gone too far into the woods when we heard a strange Bard Owl. Most Owls won't call out during the day unless something disturbs their tree. There was something off with this Owl call. It sounded 'strange, and it was much louder.

John turned to give me a knowing smile. The young were in the area. That let us know that mom and dad weren't far off. It wouldn't surprise me if we were watched the whole time. Since we had been outed, John and I headed back to the camper. We still needed to come up with a strategy.

We stayed in the camper that afternoon and John made us soup for dinner. I still wasn't feeling like myself, so this downtime was well needed. While we ate, we came up with an idea. Remove the food source. If you removed the food, it would cause any animals to move on. We just had to remove every food opportunity from the Partain's property. Then we would just have to give it time.

I was feeling good about our decision while John and I watched TV that night. He was in the recliner, and I was curled up on the couch with a blanket. I had almost fallen asleep when something hit the window right by my head causing me to jump. John immediately hit the mute button on the TV, and we listened. My heart was pounding in my chest! When we didn't hear anything else, John got up and turned on the outside light. He opened the door and looked out, but he said he didn't see anything. He turned the TV back on, and I lay back down on the couch. We had them hit the side of our camper on numerous occasions. I think they were just curious as to what we were doing inside. Usually, it was only one or two hits, and then all would be quiet.

I hadn't been asleep long when something hit the camper hard enough to shake it! I was confused when I was suddenly brought out of a deep sleep by a loud noise. John had muted the TV again and was up on his feet. Just as he started to walk over to the door, there was the most horribly loud sound I had ever heard! It was metal crunching and squealing with glass breaking. It was almost ear-splitting! What in the world was happening? We both knew what it was at the same time when the front door went dark. Something had just broken the front light! Before I could say anything, the whole camper went dark! Something had unplugged our power source! Things had just gone from bad to worse. Something had disconnected our inverter from the battery in the camper. The only way to get to this was from the outside. I didn't want John going out there. I felt like a sitting duck.

Only a few seconds had gone by when we heard the most horrible scream. This just confirmed what we already knew. It was outside the camper, and it wasn't happy with us being there.

I had heard this scream before, but it really scared me tonight standing there in the dark. I was feeling unusually vulnerable. The camper began to slowly move back and forth. To start with it was barely noticeable but then the rocking got stronger! The camper started to groan, and all of my dishes and glasses began to fall out of the cabinets breaking as they hit the floor and counters.

I let out a scream that could have rivaled a Sasquatch. I was frightened to the very core of my being. They had never done this before! The second after I screamed, the rocking stopped. The sudden silence was almost as ear-splitting as the chaos had been.

John put his arms around me to comfort me. Why had they done this? Were they trying to hurt us or scare us? I was ready to leave. I now felt like we were in over our heads.

John and I stood there in the dark for what seemed like an eternity, just waiting to see what would happen next. After some time had passed and everything was still quiet. John said, "I'm going to get the flashlight, and I'm going out to fix the inverter." I didn't want him going out there. What if it was still outside? It could easily kill him. "Please don't," I said. I was more scared than I had ever been.

"It will only take a minute," John said. "You stay here, and I will be right back."

John fumbled around the kitchen until he found the flashlight. He went out the front door and around the camper. I stood in the doorway listening for the slightest movement in the dark.

After what seemed like forever, our lights blinked back on in the camper and I could now hear the familiar hum from the refrigerator letting me know the power was back on. John hurried around the camper and back inside.

"I don't know how in the hell they did it, but they disconnected the inverter," he said. "Nothing was damaged; it was just unplugged." I could see the shock on his face. How were they smart enough to do this? Or had it just been a coincidence?

John and I cleaned up the camper and waited until the first light of dawn before trying to get any sleep. We woke to the sound of Tom's truck pulling in close to the camper.

John got up and went to the door as I got dressed. I could hear Tom saying that he thought he had better come out and check on us, that things had gotten pretty bad at his house last night.

I went into the kitchen and put on coffee as John and Tom talked. The Sasquatch had torn up a few things at Tom's place last night. He said that he had never known it to do things like this. It must not like the fact that John and I were there and in its territory. John explained to him that it was typical behavior if they felt threatened especially when they had young ones. They are just like any other animal or human. They will protect the family at all cost.

Over coffee that morning we told Tom what we planned to do. He said that now would be a perfect time since he didn't have any chickens or livestock left. We explained to him how this would not only affect him but how it could have an impact on his neighbors as well. He said that the only neighbor that was having problems was his closest neighbor Ray. We thought it would be best if we spoke with Ray as well. Tom told us to come over to his house this afternoon, and he would have Ray come over to talk to us.

John and I had our work cut out for us. But after speaking with Ray, he and Tom had agreed to help us. We would remove every food source from both their properties. John explained to them that the deer and other animals would probably move out when the Sasquatch did, and they were okay with that. We planned to begin our clearing the next day.

The next day we met at Tom's with Ray and his wife, Betty. The six of us were all equipped with clippers, shovels, and a whole array of gardening tools. We would walk the woods cutting down and digging up any fruit trees or berry bushes. Anything edible had to go.

I was exhausted after the first couple of hours. Lily and John tried to get me to go back to the camper and rest. I probably should have, but after what had happened last night, I was a little scared to be at the camper by myself. I told them that I would be fine.

It was slow going because we didn't want to miss anything and the plants were just starting to put out green leaves. If you didn't know exactly what you were looking for you could walk right over it.

By late afternoon we had worked our way down to the swamp. I had wanted to see this place. This is where Tom and Ray had run into the big guy.

Betty and Lily decided to go back and cook some dinner. They had asked me if I wanted to come along, but I was excited about seeing the swamp and the slim possibility of the mother and her young, that I told them I would stay and help out here.

There were some persimmon trees on the far side of the swamp. I had decided that I would be the one to go cut them down. I made my way around the swamp to the trees. The men were running a chainsaw and cutting through some underbrush. It had to have been the chainsaw noise that kept me from hearing the warning scream from the mother.

Without even knowing it, I had walked up on her and the two little ones. By the time I saw movement out of the corner of my eye, she was already emitting an ear-splitting screech. She stood not ten feet from me, in the shadows, just inside the tree line with a baby on her hip and two older ones on either side of her. These siblings looked to be about three feet tall, and they were both black. The two siblings dropped down on all fours and were gone in an instant. The female opened her mouth really wide and screamed again before she turned away from me and disappeared into the woods. I remember seeing something almost like fear in her eyes. I was scared to death yet I felt terrible that she had the need to fear for her young. I was just turning my head back to the Persimmon trees when something hit me in my right temple. I remember smelling something like a wet dog before everything went black and the chainsaw noise faded.

Chapter 7

I woke up with all of the men crouching down above me and a frantic John calling my name. When I sat up my head was pounding. This was the worst headache I had ever had! I reached up to rub my temple when John grabbed my hand. "Don't touch it," he said. "You have a cut there that we need to clean." As the men helped me to my feet, I remembered what happened. Something or someone had hit me. I quickly turned to look at the woods. Was it still there?!

The men helped me over to a fallen tree to sit for a minute. I was beginning to feel better. Naturally, John asked me what had happened. I don't know why, but I didn't want to say that I had gotten to close to the female and her young. So I just said that I fell. That could have been true, I had no clue what hit me in the head. I didn't see a thing.

After I got injured, the men decided to quit for the day. We had gotten most of it done anyway. It would only take another half of a day to finish up. I was more than ready to head back to the camper.

Tom invited us to come over for dinner that night. But I wasn't feeling so good. John, knowing this, told him he was going to take me home to rest. Tom agreed and said that he may come by to check on us later.

An hour later, I had a shower, some Tylenol and was on the couch with a blanket. I wanted to go to sleep. But John wanted me to stay awake for a while since I had just suffered a head injury.

John brought me a cup of hot tea and sat down across from me. With a very stern look on his face, he said, "OK, now tell me exactly what happened out there today." I knew that he would never believe the story of me falling.

I told John about seeing the small Persimmon trees and how I had gone over to cut them down. I watched the shock on his face as I said to him that I walked up on the female. The noise from the saw running had kept us both from hearing each other. She had screamed at me as a warning to back up away from her and her babies. I was in shock and apparently hadn't retreated fast enough. I told John about the tiny baby she had with her. That could explain why the male has been hunting food and has been more aggressive recently. They had three little ones now. John agreed that could explain the male's behavior. I told John about the smell just before I was hit. Just like I did, he assumed it was the male, protecting its family.

John brought me my lap top while he went to make us a quick dinner. I wanted to see if I could find anything that might help us understand what was going on and the best way to deal with it.

After John and I finished dinner, we were both tired and ready for bed. It was only around eight, but we thought the extra rest might do us good. We cleaned up the kitchen and went to bed.

Crawling into our bed felt terrific. I was sound asleep within minutes. I was even too tired to worry about the Sasquatch tonight. I just needed sleep. John must have been as tired as I was because neither of us heard the yell coming from the woods.

The second yell was closer. But neither John nor myself even moved in our sleep. The heavy Bipedal footsteps walked around the camper for a while. There was the occasional soft grunt. I'm not sure if it was checking out the camper or trying to find the way in. The camper groaned as it rocked back and forth on its frame. John nor I as much as moved. My soft breathing and Johns heavy snoring were audible on the outside recorder.

The rocking of the camper stopped, and the heavy footsteps began again. I wonder if this is because it wasn't getting a response from us. The footsteps went on for a while, and the grunts were deeper now. At one point the recorder captured something that sounded like gibberish. It seemed like someone trying to speak in a foreign tongue but way too fast.

I started to turn over in the bed, but my sore temple woke me up. I lay there for just a moment; my eyes were still shut. I repositioned myself and was drifting back off to sleep when a massive, hairy arm came crashing through the window above our bed! John and I were immediately covered with shards of Plexiglas! My eyes flew open to see this big hairy arm above me caught in the mini blinds and waving around frantically. I screamed just as John's feet hit the floor. I rolled off the bed to keep this thing from touching me! I scrambled to my feet at the same time the arm went back out the window, and the camper begins to rock. This Sasquatch let out a yell that I could feel deep within my chest. Just like a big bass drum.

The camper was rocking with such force that John and I were having a hard time staying on our feet! We were both grabbing onto the walls and door frames as we tried to make it out of the bedroom. The camper was pitch black, and the sound of glass breaking and the camper groaning was deafening! Luckily, John's gun was mounted over the bedroom door so it couldn't fall while we were traveling. John was trying to stay on his feet and release the hardware clips that held the shotgun in place. I knew that we were going to have to shoot this thing, but I wondered if it would kill it or just make it angrier. Either way, we had to do something quickly. If it turned this camper over, we could both be killed.

The camper stopped rocking, and the horrible sound of the front window breaking filled my ears. At the same second, I heard the shell engage in Johns gun. It went off with a deafening blast and a blinding flash. The creature outside let out a horrible scream and must have charged the camper. We heard the metal and steel buckle as this thing hit the area around the front door. The camper shifted back a few feet and then we were falling. The camper was turning over. I heard John scream "SUSAN! HOLD ON!" But there was nothing I could do. I fell across the kitchen table, and my feet went over my head. My whole body was being pummeled by our belongings. The camper froze for a split second in mid-air before crashing back down on its tires. The silence was eerie. Before John or I either one could speak, we heard a single gunshot. And then three more in Rapid session. I was hurting and confused. Who was shooting? Where had those shots come from? We heard the Sasquatch scream again, but this time it was at a distance. It sounded like it was headed back for the woods.

I knew I had to get up on my feet, but before that thought had left my mind, I heard Tom's voice. 'JOHN! SUSAN! ARE Y'ALL ALRIGHT IN THERE"? It was Tom! Tom was here! I slowly tried to move my legs that were now doubled under me. The pain was terrible, but I didn't think anything was broken.

"SUSAN?" John yelled from the front of the camper. "I'm OK"! I called back. I could hear Johns feet crunching on broken glass as he came toward me. "We're OK Tom!" John called out. The camper was still pitch black as John called out to me again. " Susan? Where are you?"

"Down here, I said reaching one arm out toward where I thought he was. John grabbed my hand and pulled me to my feet. My back was hurting, but I didn't think I had broken anything. John and I slowly made it over to where the front door was. We couldn't open it. It had sustained too much damage.

Someone was now shining a flashlight around the front of the camper. I could see through the rays of light just how much damage had been done. It looked like a bomb had gone off inside our camper.

Tom and John discussed getting the front door open. It was our only way out. We had two fire windows, one in the bedroom and one in the front room but both of them had been too damaged to open correctly. We needed to use the door. Tom handed John some tools through the front window. With both men working on the door it took about ten minutes to get us out. For me, this was an eternity. What if this thing came back? I knew it would kill Tom without even hesitating.

They finally got the door bent up from the floor enough for us to crawl out on our hands and knees. We all piled into Toms truck without looking back.

It was near midnight when we got back to the Partain's house. We talked for a bit over coffee, and then Lily showed us to the guest bedroom. John and I both knew that we wouldn't be sleeping for the rest of the night.

The next morning Tom and Lily drove us down to the field where our camper was. I was shocked! It looked like it had just been through a horrible wreck. The metal on the front was even bent back from the frame! It took nothing less than brute force to accomplish this.

We all got out of the truck slowly. No one knew what to say. I felt the tears come up in my eyes as I looked at what used to be my home. Then it hit me! The Sasquatch may have felt this way when we showed up here in its territory, and if that weren't bad enough, we started removing all of its food! How could we have not expected something like this?

We spent the next two days with Tom and Lily waiting for the insurance adjuster to come to look at the camper. It was completely totaled. Tom didn't offer an explanation, and the adjuster put roll over in his report. We left it at that.

I was pretty sure the adjuster knew that it wasn't a wreck, but the insurance on the camper was good so he could have cared less.

Things were quiet at the pertains house for the rest of the time we were there. We didn't know if the Sasquatch was severely injured, or if it knew it had forced us to leave and was now content with its win.

Lily and Tom followed us as we drove back out to the camper one last time. Tom had brought his chainsaw to cut the door off. Tom and I would salvage what we could, and the rest would be left behind for the tow truck to dispose of.

On my last trip out the front door. I saw the recorder hanging on the trailer hitch. I lifted it off and dropped it into my pocket. I knew it had stopped running. The batteries usually lasted about forty-eight hours. I wondered if I even wanted to hear what was on it.

John put the last box in the back of our pickup truck, and we hugged Tom and Lily. Leaving our new friends was sad. Some people you just connect with on a deeper level. And the Partain's had been those people. We promised to come back and visit them after we got a new camper.

Tom and I did get a new camper after the insurance paid off. We got one that I like better than the one we had. Thanks to the insurance policy. Knowing what we could run into, John had taken out a whopper of an insurance policy on the camper. But that was just like him, always taking care of us.

It has been over a year, and I'm thrilled to say that the Partain's have had no more activity around their house. The last walk John and I did didn't even reveal any new tree structures. The Sasquatch has moved on. We can't promise that it won't eventually come back, but for now, it's gone.

John and I still continue to help what people we can while we search for answers to our own questions. I didn't take any time off after our camper attack. I knew that if I did, I might not ever go back out. This is something I have grown to love doing, and I didn't want to lose that. But now, when convenience allows, we spend some nights in a hotel room. Especially if we know that the Sasquatch has shown signs of aggression. Live and learn.

Until next time, thank you for reading.

If you enjoyed this book, please consider leaving a review. Also, you might want to check out some of Melissa's other titles.

Bigfoot Chronicles, A true story

Bigfoot Chronicles 2, A true story

Sasquatch, The Native Truth. A true story

Sasquatch, The Native Truth. Kecleh-Kudleh Mountain A true story

Sasquatch, The Native Truth. Ravens Return A true story

The True Haunting of a Paranormal Investigator

Dog Man, A True Encounter

Black Eyed Kids. My Three Months of Hell. A true story

Family Ties Fiction

Female Bigfoot Encounters. True Stories

Our Paranormal Reality, A True Haunting. Book 1 The Early Years

Our Paranormal Reality, A True Haunting. Book 2 The Investigation

Bigfoot, A New Reality. A True Story

The Birth of a Psychic with Telekinesis. A True Story

Lifting the Veil on All Things Paranormal, True Stories

Desolate Mountain, One woman's true story of survival.

The Watcher, A true story.

Bigfoot Found me. One man's true encounter with Bigfoot.

Goodbye. A true story of a Ouija board experience

Melissa's books can be found online at
Amazon
Barnes and Noble
Books a Million
Wal-Mart
and your local bookstore.

Follow Melissa on,

Her Blog;
http://www.melissageorge.net/

Facebook;
https://www.facebook.com/AuthorMelissaGeorge/

Twitter;
https://twitter.com/MelissaDGeorge

Google;
https://plus.google.com/+MelissaGAuthor

Pinterest;
https://www.pinterest.com/melissa6144/

Instagram;
https://www.instagram.com/melissageorge_paranormalauthor/r

About the Author.

Melissa was born and raised in a small town in upstate South Carolina. She first became a well-known Blogger and later decided to take her writing a step further. Her first book, My Paranormal Life, A True Haunting started out as her own private journal of her family dealing with a dark entity. But it doesn't stop there, Melissa took it even further and let her experiences help her to co-found a paranormal team and a cryptid team. She enjoys being able to reach out and help others. She has made many new friends in both of these fields, which has also led her to help others to have their story told. Melissa realizes first hand that these people have a very passionate and unique story that needs to be told. In getting these powerful stories out to the public, she hopes it will help further research in both of these fields, and just maybe the individual that shares their story with her may find some closure to their own personal nightmare. Melissa feels honored to be able to bring you true stories of the unexplained.

Made in the USA
Las Vegas, NV
28 December 2023

83604241R00080